the fairest tax

RENDERING
unto CAESAR

ROBERT L. SAVAGE

the fairest tax

RENDERING
unto CAESAR

ROBERT L. SAVAGE

TATE PUBLISHING & *Enterprises*

Published by Tate Publishing & Enterprises, LLC
127 E. Trade Center Terrace | Mustang, Oklahoma 73064 USA
1.888.361.9473 | www.tatepublishing.com

Tate Publishing is committed to excellence in the publishing industry. The company reflects the philosophy established by the founders, based on Psalm 68:11,
"The Lord gave the word and great was the company of those who published it."

Book design copyright © 2011 by Tate Publishing, LLC. All rights reserved.
Cover design by Kristen Verser
Interior design by Chelsea Womble

Published in the United States of America

ISBN: 978-1-61346-314-7
1. Business & Economics, Taxation, General
2. Business & Economics, Government & Business
11.08.04

Dedicated to Annette
My wife, whom I love now and for always!

TABLE OF CONTENTS

PREFACE

Almost 235 years ago, our nation's founders determined that inaction was no longer an option. Because much of the reason for this included a serious and growing mistrust of their government's officials, they knew that whatever was needed, they would have to be the ones to do it. Such important matters could no longer be entrusted to officials—no matter how well intentioned some of those persons might be—who were so subject to the corrupting influences of power and special interest groups.

Realizing this, they acted. And from their action was born what is now universally accepted to be one of the single greatest advances in human civilization.

Out of this "American Miracle of 1776" came the United States of America with a form of government so well thought out and designed—taking from the world's experience up to that time the best features of previous governments and prohibiting the damaging excesses of others—that it could say its goal was to secure for its citizens the rights to "life, liberty and the pursuit of happiness."

Clearly the American documents—the Declaration of Independence and the Constitution of the United

States of America—that were produced were unbeliev-ably far-sighted. While there were some serious flaws (such as failing to abolish slavery and not granting women the right to vote), the ideals and form of gov-ernment they established have since proven the wisdom of the founders who designed and wrote them, as well as the citizens who subsequently debated and approved them.

Much of that wisdom was embodied in the clear recognition that even they could not address at that time all the flaws or foresee all the possible future needs of their new nation. Thus, they made sure to include the vital capabilities needed to allow future citizens to amend their constitution should it become necessary.

Now, as we have entered a new millennia, all of us as citizens of the United States seem to be facing another time such as that of our founders. We find that we are again facing huge questions about how much we can trust our government officials. While we still see the great wisdom in our republican form of gov-ernment compared to any other, we also find that too often the corrupting influences of such great power on those who occupy even its minor positions—let alone its major offices—seem to prevent us from growing to our greatest potential. *Even after we debate and elect our officials with clear mandates on things like term limits and true political campaign reform, we still cannot get action from our politicians. Then adding to this, we keep finding more and more new instances of massive personal data files being kept (and too often mishandled) on more and more of us as individual citizens.*

It seems that no matter who from among us we elect or appoint, the ultimate outcomes raise more and more doubts about our government officials' ability to withstand the lure of the powers they are given. Even the most honest and well intentioned of those we elect too soon seem to change from statesmen and stateswomen into mere incumbent politicians.

Sometimes the pressure of special interest groups with vast amounts of money is just too great. Or maybe it is the lure of favors and ego-strokes from high-paid lobbyists who seem to be less-than-caring for the truth.

Maybe it is the unparalleled influence of our media who we would like to depend on. But instead we see reporters and editors who seem anything but unbiased, or simply catering to deep-pocket advertisers whose messages no longer appear trustworthy.

Looking back, we inherently sense that our founders were mostly comprised of statesmen rather than professional politicians.

Today, it seems that our system—with all of its marvelous and major strengths—does have at least a few areas where *we citizens must again take action. It is simply too difficult to envision that under today's circumstances, enough of our politicians can ever find the necessary will and resolve to sacrifice even some of their acquired power and position.*

Of course, our current need for citizen action is much more complex than just reestablishing the dominance of the "statesman" and "stateswoman" within our government. For such a large effort, a new 1776-Style Continental Convention will likely be necessary. But we can also chip away with specific proposals and thus begin reversing the debilitating course we have been on far too long.

In this spirit, it seems very timely for one "ordinary" citizen to offer an idea that all "ordinary" citizens of this marvelous nation can use to debate. Then, if we think it wise, we can act (using the very process and flexibility built into our constitution) to improve (or perhaps even reclaim) a very important part of our rights to life, liberty, and the pursuit of happiness.

The *idea* in this instance is one I firmly believe would dramatically improve our nation by introducing a far more efficient and fairer system of paying for our government. It would do this by bringing in elements that (1) reward the best character traits of citizens; (2) reduce the continual impositions of governmental demands for exhausting amounts of personal information and even its well-intentioned (but too often over-burdening) rules and regulations on individuals and businesses; and (3) allow domestic organizations to compete far better with foreign nations who are currently taking away jobs and trade that should remain within our own borders.

It would also vastly simplify our tax system and require our governments to be honest and straightforward about all the costs they incur and the ways they charge us for their services.

If this idea seems valid to you, a major caveat must be remembered. Each reader should recognize the lack of perfect, or even very profound, knowledge by the author.

This short book and its concept comes from more than two years of effort in the early 1990s to conceive a tax system that will work—while at the same time be both understandable and considered "fair" by the great majority of our fellow citizens. It is from someone who deeply loves our great nation and has enjoyed a varied and productive life in the military, several businesses, numerous states, and both large and small communities.

My hope is only that this book and its concept will contribute something of lasting value to this marvelous nation that I and so many of us love so deeply and owe so much.

Finally, my resume includes experiences, which though extremely useful, do not make one an expert on so complex a subject. Yet it just may be that what this nation now needs most is fewer professionals, intellectuals, and experts, and more plain citizens who are less concerned with detailed and complex systems and more interested in approaches that simply make sense.

Experiences which have led to the ideas expressed in this book include:

- Formal education up through and including a Master's degree
- Four years of active military service
- Business management experience for almost 30 years with a very large company including:

  —both line and staff responsibilities

  —extensive dealings with other large firms

  —extensive dealings with numerous federal and state government agencies

  —extensive work with legal groups

- Ownership and active management experience for almost 20 years of a very small (and successful) business

- Extensive work in the fields of engineering, marketing, economics and business administration

- Numerous places of residence and work including over 3 years in Washington, DC

One thing is for sure; it is extremely unlikely that our nation's forefathers (and foremothers) had in mind the unbelievable amounts and types of intrusions into our citizens' lives that exist today. Very little imagination is needed to understand what they most wanted.

It seems they simply desired two things from their new government:

1. protection from outside attacks by empire-building foreigners or by unhappy Native Americans

2. assurance that their various states would work together to promote—or at least not impede—trade and enterprise between each other.

In short, what they wanted most was a federal government designed to allow them to live in relative safety while individually pursuing happiness and a livelihood for themselves and their families.

They also understood that they would have to pay for that government. If they decided on a small amount of government the required payments would be less, but if they opted for more services, the amount of taxes they paid would have to be larger. They seem to have decided to be very stingy in giving up their hard-earned money to their new federal government.

They did not opt for guarantees or "entitlements," but instead appear to have wanted only a peaceful land with "individual opportunity."

They also decided that their new government's revenues should come largely from sources like tariffs on goods coming into the country from the outside world rather than taxes on property and incomes that potentially affected their personal wealth or incentives to build the nation. Then—when this was not enough—they turned to the wealthiest for either loans or gifts.

Today, we can learn a great deal from these folks' experience and wisdom. Looking at their actions, we can deduce that we should revisit our current system and revamp it.

An essential premise for this volume is the fact that how much we pay is almost completely separate from the method by which we pay. *Thus, it concerns only how we should be taxed.*

17.10.1—40.22.17

OVERVIEW

It's simple! Try as we might, the only honest conclusion is that *we must pay for our government.*

How much we must pay depends on how much we want our government to do. If we decide on a small amount of government, our required payments will be less. If we conclude that more government services are desired, the amount of taxes we must pay will have to be larger.

Since we must pay, *we should demand several things from the system or process used by our government officials* to determine how and when we are taxed. We should require at least the following:

1. The entire system should be a *single* process requiring our various governments to *clearly* state in one bill the *total* amount of all tax revenues they require to operate.

2. The way we each pay should be *simple* and *straightforward* without complex rules and the loopholes that inevitably result from even the best intended of such rules. And there should *never* be a requirement for any government body to hold massive or other files of personal data on the vast majority of us—its individual citizens.

3. Our tax system should work in a way that *those of us with the most pay the greatest amounts*. It

should operate so that *everyone* pays, including today's so-called underground economy or citizens who do not report income from illegal sources. It should even include legal and illegal foreigners living within our borders.

4.   Our tax system should *encourage* those of us with less to build and accumulate greater financial resources. Then it should *allow* us to pass on to our children without penalties what we have built and accumulated. It should *facilitate* citizens and families who wish to do so to more easily join the ranks of the wealthy.

5.   Finally, where businesses and all other non-person organizations are concerned, our tax system should *encourage* them to provide us with good jobs plus desirable products and services. It should also *function to level the playing field* between small or startup efforts versus giant firms with tremendous economic advantages. It should not be designed—as ours is today—in a way that encourages foreign corporations to send huge untaxed profits made in our nation to their home country.

Such a system would be by far the least intrusive on each citizen's freedom and at the same time the most fair way for each of us to pay our own share of government's costs. It should not require complex tax forms and massive personal information disclosures. Yet it should both allow us to easily see in one place how much of our money our various government bodies are spending and promote large and small businesses and organizations to produce good jobs as well as the consumer products and services we need and want in our lives.

Can such a tax system be designed and set up, and can we change to it? The clear answer to both questions is *yes! A transition that is fair, easy-to-understand, and leaves prices we pay essentially unchanged can be done over a short span of four years.*

Our new tax approach will completely replace all existing federal, state, and local tax laws and regulations (including income taxes, property taxes, estate taxes, and other "hidden" taxes and fees) as well as virtually any other significant form of government revenue.

In place of all of today's federal, state, and local taxes and revenues, it will put into service a two-part system for the vast majority of us. A third part will also be required but will apply only to our wealthiest citizens plus our biggest businesses and organizations.

The first two parts or components of our new tax approach and their roles will be:

1. The *National Dues* component will require every federal, state, and local government official to clearly establish by late summer their next year's operating budget into a single statement and per capita amount. This will allow us as citizens to much more easily see for ourselves what they do and how much they cost. We will even be able to compare our own local and state governments' efficiency and effectiveness with other similar cities and states, and vote accordingly the next time our own officials run for reelection.

   For each city or county, this budget plus each local citizen's per capita share of their state's budget and their individual share of the federal budget will be added together to determine their dues for the coming year. This amount will be the same for each of us in any given locality and will be our personal fair share of the costs our federal, state, and local governments require to do the things we want of them.

Finally, each of us as taxpayers will be able to reduce our own year's dues amount to zero simply by the everyday things we each do to provide ourselves and our families such basics as food and housing. *Very few individuals will ever owe any of their or their family's dues, and* if they want, *they can* even use volunteer service to *get a refund* early in the following year.

2. The *National Sales Tax* component will replace today's local and widely varying sales tax codes with a single straightforward percentage. This new percentage will apply evenly throughout the nation for most goods and services we, our businesses, and all other organizations (including government bodies) each buy or rent for ultimate consumption[1].

---

1   Throughout this article the assumption is made that all states and local governments will adopt matching systems and fully participate with the new federal tax system. While this is not a certainty, incentives—including no distributions from the High Revenues fund and no refunds to their citizens–should sufficiently encourage the great majority to cooperate. Should a state choose to not participate, that portion of the nationwide percentage resulting from the federal budget process will still apply. Also, products sold to sellers in those states will be subject to tariff-like charges designed to level the playing field with sellers in participating states.

No sales taxes will apply to basic living needs such as grocery staples, rent, mortgages, education, healthcare, and insurance plus goods bought by a farm or business for resale or use as material in an agricultural or manufacturing process.

By collecting our taxes this way, today's most complex activities, such as payroll withholding and complicated tax forms, will be eliminated. Existing government tax collectors, such as those in the Internal Revenue Service plus all state and local tax operations, will no longer be needed. Even tax appraisers with the judgmental and often questionable valuations they assign to our houses and property will have no part to play in our new tax approach.

The many individuals and businesses that now pay little or no income, property, or other taxes will pay this National Sales Tax along with the rest of us. Whether these non-taxpayers now avoid their payments though legal or illegal methods will no longer matter. People who simply do not file tax returns, foreigners, illegal immigrants, others in the underground economy and even felons will now have to pay their share of the National Sales Tax.

Revenues will flow steadily to our governments within the days and months following our various purchases. To a very large extent the taxes each of us pays for our purchases will quickly flow back to the locale where we live or buy the items we need and want.

While at first the new National Sales Tax percentage will seem very high compared to today's widely varying rates, the *total prices we pay now* (i.e.—the business's price plus current sales tax amount) *will not actually change very much and should even be lowered*. Because each business will quickly begin to experience greatly reduced overhead costs from our governments (such as license fees and inventory taxes) as well as their suppliers, their part of the total price of each item or service sold will quickly fall to much lower levels. Their lower prices will then offset the higher sales tax percentage.

Perhaps the most important aspect of all is the fact that our governments will no longer have any need to know or keep files about individual law-abiding citizens, except for the wealthiest and most powerful few persons, families, and organizations. Only for the few of us and our organizations who possess the most and therefore the greatest powers for mischief (as well as for good) will there be any need to know how much we earn, what we own, or other such highly personal information.

The third and last component of our new tax approach will be paid only by those of us who are the very wealthiest of individuals and families. It will also apply to our larger businesses and organizations, including those with established foreign ties.

3. The *High Revenue Tax* will require each individual and family with the largest of incomes and wealth (i.e. incomes and wealth far greater than that needed to live very comfortably) to pay this additional tax equal to an increasing percentage of all their annual revenue from *any* source.

    For these few individuals and their families, the High Revenue Tax will be in addition to their National Dues and National Sales Tax payments. It will apply to all income plus other cash and equivalent payments received or earned by their investments and activities during the year that are over and above an amount well above comfortable living standards. This amount will be $100,000.00 initially but will be reset every third year by an independent panel of economics experts who will determine the appropriate level needed to provide a very comfortable living while effectively curbing any excessive economic power that would otherwise be gained by our wealthiest individuals and families.

To help ensure that self-employed individuals plus small businesses and organizations can continue to start up and compete with our larger firms and those from foreign countries, this tax will also apply to all larger businesses and organizations. It will begin at higher levels of annual sales plus revenues from any other sources such as earnings from subsidiaries and investments.

This larger level of revenues will include *only* three types of deductions.

The first type is the total domestic cost of goods sold or the cost of all domestic goods and materials used by a farmer or manufacturer.[2] *No*

---

2   One exception must exist to this requirement regarding supplies which are domestic (i.e. totally produced within the United States). This single exception will apply only to raw materials such as crude oil or a particular metal ore which an appropriate independent panel of experts agree is *not* available in sufficient amounts in this country. As an example in an area of vital importance to us as a nation, a certain grade of crude oil that is available for drilling (even at higher cost) in this country will mean that foreign supplies of that type would not be a deductible business expense for an oil company *unless* these domestic sources were unavailable for recovery because of environmental restrictions at the site where they would have to be mined.

deduction will be allowed for any such foreign costs in their business. This will promote more use of our domestic suppliers, as well as greatly reduce the ability of foreign firms (and domestic firms with foreign subsidiaries, operations, or other ties) to avoid taxes by transferring profits made in this country to another nation.

The second type of allowed deduction will help create more jobs and job skills in this country. Annual domestic pay, up to $70,000.00 per employee (plus certain tuition and training costs) may be used to reduce an individual's or organization's High Revenue Taxes.

The third type of allowed deduction is the total of contributions given to any bona-fide churches and legitimate education or other charities.

The rules that apply to businesses will also have to apply to the largest of other organizations, such as associations, churches, and charities. Even governments will have to pay on revenues from sources other than National Dues, sales, and high revenues taxes.

Although most of us would wish it to be otherwise, there are two very strong reasons for this requirement. First, the financial operations of the largest organizations and their very great influence on political matters is essentially the same as that of our larger businesses. Second, these organizations often use their resources and facilities in ways that, though useful and even desirable, allow them to unfairly compete with otherwise good (usually small or startup) individual endeavors and businesses.

This new tax approach must have all three components. It will not work if we allow our politicians and special interest groups to alter or eliminate any of these parts.

The major reason all three components must be included is the fact that no one or two parts can accomplish all that is needed. Also, they are interrelated in important ways such as the necessity for the yearly budgeting process required in the National Dues component to set the National Sales Tax percentage.

The fact that no one component can meet all our tax system requirements can be seen in the following few examples:

- The National Dues component can force our various government officials to let us know clearly and in comparable statements how much they actually cost us. But it cannot raise the needed funds by itself without those who can least afford it paying far too much.

- The National Sales Tax will result in each citizen's and visitor's tax amounts occurring in much more direct proportion to their ability to pay.

- Only a National Sales Tax will result in payments where the government does not need to know how much most of us earns or has. In addition, so many people who—under all of today's systems—simply do not play by the rules will now have to pay along with the rest of us.

- Only a High Revenue Tax component can limit government files full of highly personal information to the *small number of individuals and organizations* with great wealth and influence and cause them to pay the even greater amounts they can afford beyond their obligations under the National Dues and National Sales Tax parts.

- Only the High Revenue Tax can limit the otherwise ever-increasing power and influence of extremely wealthy individuals, families, and organizations so that small businesses, little churches, and more local charities can continue to exist along with them.

One very good feature of the three components working together can be seen in the way they will encourage each of us to achieve and retain as much of the economic part of our "American Dream" as we individually desire.

Our poorest citizens and those just starting to build their personal wealth will be aided by the first two components. They will pay sales taxes on a much smaller portion of their purchases and even be able to earn a National Dues refund.

As individuals and families wish to and are able to build their financial resources up to middle or average levels, the National Sales Tax component will increase their total taxes while staying within their now increased ability to pay. The National Dues credits will encourage these average income citizens to begin investing and saving in ways that will further increase their education levels and wealth while also leading to better health and retirement plans.

Finally, many of us may never desire to continue accumulating ever-greater wealth, and will be able to find personal happiness and financial security at this middle or average income level. But others will want to build even greater wealth, and unlike their situation under today's tax plans, they will be far more able to do so. However, as their financial ability to pay grows, so will their total tax payments because of the increased effects of the National Sales Tax on their larger purchases and the High Revenue Tax on their larger incomes as exemplified by the chart below[3].

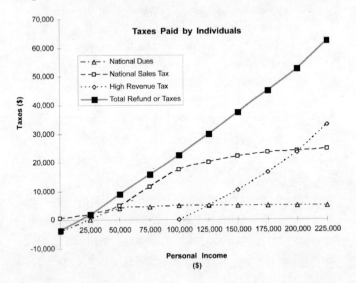

Taxes Paid by Individuals

In summary, our new tax approach offers us as individuals and organizations a far simpler and much fairer process designed to:

1. Virtually eliminate the need for our federal, state, and local governments to keep such massive amounts of personal files and information on each of us.

2. Eliminate withholdings on all but the very wealthiest among us.

---

3   The reader should not try to use this chart to estimate the actual amounts due under our new tax approach. Its purpose is to illustrate the general effects of the three components and how they will work together.

3. Consolidate all the myriad types of taxes from all our governments into one clear and comparable statement and—for the vast majority of us—only two types of taxes.

4. Vastly simplify the unbelievable maze of current federal, state, and local tax rules and regulations—many of which include questionable judgment calls by assessors, often conflict with one another, and frequently make us pay large sums to government bodies where we have no vote.

5. Result in those of us who can afford more paying more while our lower-income citizens can actually earn refunds.

For our federal, state, and local governments, this different tax process has many major advantages as well. For example, they will:

6. Receive their funds almost immediately.

7. Require smaller staffs and far less costs to handle tax filings, questions and collections.

8. Collect taxes from currently non-taxpaying groups such as illegal aliens, criminals, and people who do not report all of their taxable income.

Only two things will show up as problems when we seriously debate moving to our new tax approach.

The first of these is the simple fact that this new approach represents a significant change in how we pay for our governments. Each of us knows that no matter how open-minded we want to be, our very human resistance to change will still cause us to postpone adopting new ways. However, overcoming this problem is totally within us individually and as a nation. Once we begin serious study and debate of the need for and the change itself, we can overcome this inertia on our own.

The second problem cannot be solved without a citizenry that is solidly united in its determination to overcome the objections, delaying tactics (often called "gridlock" in today's political arenas) and ultimate attempts that will be made to literally sabotage this change. Ironically (and sadly) these objections, delays, and attempts to sabotage will come primarily from current and would-be politicians and government bureaucrats. Unfortunately, they will have lots of help from the largest businesses, foreigners, and other special interests groups (and their armies of lobbyists)—all of whom benefit from the extreme complexities of today's myriad of taxes[4].

Fortunately, the Constitution of the United States of America is very far-sighted and provides a way for its ordinary citizens to create such changes without relying on Congress. Revolts and other revolutionary means are neither

---

4   A detailed discussion of this writer's view on why and how this will occur is presented in a separate Addendum 1 at the end of this volume. It is done this way because the ideas presented there reflect very poorly on the current state of our nation's ability to be served by its government officials. That negative situation—while extremely real (though fortunately fixable) and its resultant indictment of today's "official" leadership—contrasts very sharply with the abundant optimism still deserved by this great nation and the opportunities it continues to provide its citizens. Thus, discussing this current problem in a totally separate addendum will hopefully preserve the very real optimism this writer believes should exist for the main body of this volume.

*needed nor desirable. True resolve by citizens will be needed,
and in this instance certainly demands that we proceed with
great determination no matter what enticements or theatrics
our government officials and special interest groups offer.*

Any such enticements or promised action may be
allowed to proceed but only in parallel with separate
citizen action and under the most skeptical scrutiny
possible. Otherwise, such enticements or promises will
surely turn into sham procedural or legislative changes.
Current politicians, bureaucrats, and special interest
groups have learned far better than we want to believe
how to make laws and regulations that appear one
way but in reality work to those groups' advantage and
completely differently than advertised.

Because this change is likely only through citizen action, a proposed constitutional amendment is
included as Addendum 2. While not written by a law-
yer or constitutional expert, *no changes can be permitted
in the event it is considered by our Congress or other governmental body.* Their motives can only be overwhelm-
ingly slanted against the new tax system and its seeming
dilution of their current powers. For this reason alone,
we must not accept from them anything less than the
exact wording presented in this volume's Addendum 2.

*If this amendment is adopted by citizen-only action,
Addendum 2 should provide an extremely adequate document
for debate. Thus, changes could be considered and would be
acceptable then so long as there are serious statesman-like
debates without partisan political considerations.*[5]

---

5   Actually this writer would prefer this since no claim can be
made for error-less thinking while this volume was being written.

Underlying Concepts

National Dues

One of the first and most important ideas to grasp is that very few individuals will owe any National Dues payment at the end of a tax year!

In general, only the wealthiest of individuals living in this country will ever pay any National Dues because:

1. Virtually all revenues received by our various governmental bodies will come from sales taxes and from High Revenue Taxes.

2. National Dues estimates for each of us will allow everyone to see and understand better the total amounts and the line-item parts that our governments cost each of us. Today's budget pronouncements by multitudes of government bodies, plus the sheer number of different types of taxes and other kinds of hidden charges, simply do not permit us to see how much we are paying. Once this becomes clearer to us as individual citizens, we will be far better informed and able to elect officials at every level of government who will not be inclined to the kinds

of wasteful spending that current budgets are often accused of harboring.

3. Credits available to each person will allow us and our families (who will be able to pool their dues and credits) to end up owing nothing in this area. For the poorest of our citizens, these credits can actually generate a refund through volunteer work that helps others—or when their children stay in school. For the rest of our citizens who are fortunate enough to have already accumulated more substantial financial resources, these credits will be less effective in creating a refund. However, they will allow any otherwise required National Dues payments to be eliminated through the investments these persons and families will be encouraged to make. In turn, these investments will create more jobs, encourage additional education, and provide for their own future security so that they will not be dependent on their children or our government in their elder years.

Almost everyone understands the fact that we who live in the United States are clearly among the most fortunate persons to have ever lived on this planet. We can therefore easily realize and accept that such a fantastic privilege should carry with it some dues.

National Dues Credits

The primary idea behind the National Dues credits is the fact that there are many factors driving our nation and its economy that we as individuals have little or no chance to influence. However, we can each make a difference by simply conducting our own affairs in ways that take care of our own personal needs.

In the most blunt of viewpoints, if we each take care of our own basic needs for food, shelter, clothing, and medical care, our families and our society will have far fewer burdens and costs of doing these things for us. In a more positive vein, far more human energy and resources will be available to help continually improve the living standards for everyone, especially those who truly need assistance.

In short, if more of us can and do take care of our own needs, then far more can be done to help those few who actually need assistance. It can be done with far fewer resources and at lower total costs being placed on each of us as taxpayers.

We can also help with our volunteer efforts so that tax revenue needs can be further minimized. For example, when individuals or groups provide their personal time and efforts to assist the homeless at soup kitchens, fewer tax dollars are required for those needs to be met. Likewise, when volunteers work in our public schools or to clean our environment of litter, less public money has to be raised.

Quite apart from the economic and taxpayer benefits of this kind of volunteer effort is the tremendous increase those who perform this work gain in feelings of usefulness and personal satisfaction. Also, this approach (as well as any other process that reduces the need to raise public revenues) benefits us as a nation by decreasing the amounts of money handled by individual officials and bureaucrats. Not only does it leave more money in the private sector of our economy, it also simply reduces the opportunities for graft and mishandling of those funds by public officials.

Finally, as our individual work efforts begin to create greater returns, our personal income and wealth will normally increase to the point where we will start to make investments beyond basic savings accounts. These more powerful types of investments include such things as stocks, bonds, mutual funds, real estate, and even our own small business ventures. They will not only provide us individually with greater financial security. They will also add economic strength to our nation by creating still more jobs for fellow citizens.

Much the same also can be said for three other types of *investments* that can be used to create credits toward our own National Dues. The first are the wages and tips that we individually pay to others who do work for us or who perform services such as waiters and waitresses at the restaurants we visit. Our payments of this sort contribute to their incomes just as does the paycheck of anyone employed at a factory or a local department store.

The second other type of *investments* consists of payments made by us or our families for an individual's education. These payments lead to extremely valuable returns for us as individuals and as a nation because the amount of someone's education so often coincides very strongly with the amount of financial success and personal fulfillment they attain in life.

Finally, our contributions to bona-fide churches and charities should be recognized as the third other type of *investments* benefiting our nation.

For designing our tax system, these concepts provide incentives as follows:

(1) Things that can be done by any citizen regardless of personal incomes or other financial means.

    (a) Acting positively in ways that take care of our own basic needs and those of our own family.

    (b) Giving our personal time and efforts to help others who truly need assistance.

    (c) Working to aid our society in more general ways that can reduce our governments' need for additional taxes.

(2) Things that can be done to a much greater extent only after we as individuals or through our families have built up personal income or wealth.

    (a) Paying wages and tips to others and investing in things that create jobs.

    (b) Paying costs associated with our education and that of family members or others we may be able to assist.

    (c) Contributing to charities and charitable endeavors such as educational scholarships.

In addition to the economic and tax benefits from these credits or incentives, each of these types of actions will undoubtedly build our individual self-esteem and personal confidence. *In the longer term, this could turn out to be the biggest boost of all to our nation.*

National Sales Tax

Probably the most important idea to consider about using a sales tax plan to pay for the cost of our government is that those who can most afford to do so will pay the greatest share by a wide margin.

Also, while the new percentages will seem very high, they will apply to much lower prices, and we will most often pay these sales taxes at those times and places of our own choosing.

However, it is also very important to understand another companion idea. A sales tax plan's greatest weakness is the fact that our governments' income will always drop during economic downturns or war.

For such times—when we often need more public spending—we must have some "savings" available to overcome these drops. In other words *adequate reserve funds previously established and maintained by our public officials must be available.*

A National Sales Tax plan includes many desirable features.

1. It will produce revenues almost immediately when we make purchases for our personal or businesses' consumption. *This essentially wipes out any need for withholdings from the paychecks of the vast majority of us.*

2. To a very large extent, our taxable purchases will be made only in amounts and at the times that we as individual consumers (and now tax-payers) choose.

3. Not only will each of us pay in proportion to the amounts of goods and services we and our businesses consume, but so will our tourists, legal immigrants, and foreign nationals living or visiting in our country and even illegal immigrants among us. Further, citizens who cheat today and do not pay their shares of income

and other taxes will have to pay sales taxes like the rest of us. Even those whose incomes come from illegal acts such as bank robbery and drug trafficking will have to pay sales taxes on the things they purchase.

4. Sales taxes will be collected by our legitimate businesses just as they are today *and will not require each of us to submit highly personal and private information on ourselves or our families.* In fact, our government officials will have no reason to know who paid or how much any of us paid throughout a year!

5. Sales tax codes will be extremely simple compared to today's systems with their complex rules and ever-changing regulations that most of us find too confusing to use effectively. Items that we wish to buy will either be taxable or not, and the business from whom we are considering making that purchase will be able to tell us which is the case *before* we decide to buy.

6. Sales taxes cannot be hidden as are so many of our governments' taxes at the present time. A tax equal to a percentage of the price charged by a merchant in a competitive business is very straightforward compared to a franchise tax on one's cable television bill or an Emergency 911 charge on our telephone statement each month.

7. Sales taxes eliminate the unfair aspects of charges, such as the 911 fees that end up being billed *only* to local paying telephone customers, even though the government's emergency response operations and costs are the result of *all* citizens plus the area's tourists and visitors.

8. Sales taxes eliminate the judgmental character of such things as property taxes, where another

human being decides the value of your house or farm to calculate how much you will be assessed. Sales taxes actually eliminate the need for that public official and any reason to even keep files with that type of personal information at all. They would always be based only on the price that is paid for a product or service.

9. A National Sales Tax plan will effectively sanction the considerable amount of bartering that goes on today as part of the often discussed underground economy. Such activity, which was so much a legitimate part of the lives of our early citizens, would actually be encouraged. This differs from today's rules that often make bartering a taxable event, even though it is virtually unenforceable. Only that barter activity where the prices that would have otherwise applied are clearly free of judgment calls by unnecessary government officials or rules will be subject to the sales tax. This includes only barter transactions where at least one party is a businessperson or other legal entity whose prices in a non-barter situation could be easily determined.

10. A National Sales Tax will virtually eliminate much of our present underground economy's ability to avoid paying taxes. It will help honest taxpayers who sometimes simply do not know whether an action in which they were involved is or is not taxable. This alone will eliminate most of the questions and sometimes dirty feelings we can experience under today's complex codes.

11. A sales tax plan that is national will rid this country of those distasteful cases where we are often charged higher than normal tax amounts

simply because the local government officials know we have no alternative. No longer will we prepare to check out of a hotel in a large city or a tourist town only to discover that the local and state officials require that establishment to add extra high tax charges to our bill. Today, these can often run up the amount of our bill by 15 percent and more compared to the rates quoted to us earlier when we made our reservation or checked in.

12. A National Sales Tax plan will eliminate tremendous amounts of government duplicity. No longer will a state or city where we have no vote be able to assess very large taxes on our income or property as happens now when we work or own real estate in a locale other than the one where we reside[6]. Instead, our taxes will be paid to the places where we spend our time and efforts. For example, a family who owns a second home will be taxed by that state and city very much in proportion to the amount of time they spend in that area.

13. A National Sales Tax plan will prevent such questionable practices used by many states and cities today as taxing nonresidents' income earned in their jurisdiction or attempting to tax a retiree's income after that person has moved

---

6   Allowing so many types of taxes to occur in cases where *the paying citizen does not have a vote* (like income tax in a state where one works, but does not reside or property taxes on land owned in a county where one grew up but no longer lives) seems to this writer to contrast very sharply with the wisdom of our forefathers who held the Boston Tea Party and other such events because of their *strong protests against "taxation without representation."*

to another part of the nation. When we cannot vote in that jurisdiction, does not this amount to "taxation without representation"?

14. A National Sales Tax rate may seem very high by today's experience, but even that fact will have significant advantages to us as consumers and as a nation. This high tax rate will make us far better consumers. Such large amounts added to our purchases will force us to consider the real price before we buy. It will force our businesses to always tell us the real price, which is the merchant's amount plus the sales tax. This is vastly different from today's misleading environment where consumers seldom ask, and the businesses[7] from whom we buy seldom quote anything but their portion of the actual price. Just before we switch to a National Sales Tax plan, the basic prices charged by merchants, service companies, and virtually anyone with whom we consider giving our business will have to start falling drastically. This must happen simply because so many of the overhead costs they have today (which they must recover through present price levels) are much higher than their new overheads will be after the elimination of the heavy load of government taxes and fees now in effect. Then, as more time passes, they should continue to fall—although more slowly. As this process unfolds, the new total price of many goods and services (which we now know

---

7   A notable—and refreshing—exception for most of us today is our local gas station where normally the pump price already includes all the taxes that will apply when we buy a gallon of fuel. This practice would become the standard way of pricing under our National Sales Tax plan.

consists of the seller's price plus the higher sales tax) will likely return to the same approximate levels as today's total amounts (including current sales tax rates).

15. A true National Sales Tax plan will eliminate most of the border differences, where a business in one city must add that locale's tax rate (say 8 percent) to their products, while their competitor located only a block away but just outside that jurisdiction must add only the county tax rate (say 5 percent) to the same item. Because that difference can be very significant on a large item's price, the competitor outside the city has a distinct advantage today. Eliminating the city merchant's disadvantage will give us more choices as consumers.

16. A National Sales Tax plan will cause much more real competition to occur, which will also be a positive force to drive consumer prices down. Today, many individuals would like to open new businesses in markets where our current tax systems actually create an *un-level playing field*. This prevents many new competitors from opening otherwise good businesses and deprives us as consumers of many potential new choices. For example, it is often the case that a privately run daycare cannot compete with a similar operation run by a church. The church pays none of the property taxes that the private owner would face. The same is often true where the private daycare operation would like to locate close to a YMCA, which faces a vastly smaller set of governmental costs because it is a *nonprofit* organization.

Most of the advantages listed above will happen simply by changing to a National Sales Tax plan. Some of them, however, require that other steps be accomplished together with the change to the National Sales Tax.

These other actions that must be done simultaneously with the start of our new tax plan are actually very desirable to us as citizens and taxpayers. They include *eliminating all other types of taxes and "hidden" or different government assessments*[8] such as:

- Income taxes (federal, state, and local)
- Property taxes (real and intangible)
- Estate and inheritance taxes
- Existing sales taxes
- Business income and net worth taxes
- Social Security and Medicare taxes
- Unemployment taxes (federal, state, and local)
- Workers' compensation insurance requirements
- "Hidden" taxes such as franchise fees on cable television bills and 911 assessments on telephone statements
- Business license fees.

---

8 Throughout this book the assumption is made that all states and local governments will adopt matching systems and fully cooperate/participate with the new federal tax system. While this is probably not a sure thing, incentives—including no distributions from the High Revenues fund and no refunds to their citizens–should sufficiently encourage the great majority to cooperate.

One other action must also be taken with the establishment of a true National Sales Tax plan. It is absolutely necessary to offset the plan's greatest weakness. Without it, a National Sales Tax plan would be just another complication in today's already overly complex tax system.

Concurrent with the switch to the new tax approach, our federal government and each state and local government must be required to establish and adequately fund their own *reserve* for use only during times of economic downturns or war. During such times, sales tax revenues will fall below budget levels, but government appropriations remain necessary while the economy recovers or our nation defends itself.

During economic hard times—which cannot be declared by government officials but only by an independent panel of randomly chosen experts in economics—these reserve tax dollars will be released for use as the elected officials direct. Then, as soon as economic activity reaches an appropriate stage of recovery (as determined again by an independent panel of experts) or the war is over, these elected officials will be required to begin replenishing their electorate's reserve.

During times of conflict with other entities outside our nation, these reserves will be released only when war is declared by Congress.

High Revenue Tax

Each of us as individual taxpayers has likely wondered why we so often hear of very wealthy individuals and large corporations who pay little or no taxes in any given year. Looking at our own tax bills, that question can be particularly perplexing. When we really think about it, we realize that these investors and business endeavors provide us with the jobs we need plus the goods and services we want in our daily routines. Thus, in most cases, their investments and businesses would be desirable *even if they paid no taxes at all.*

If we continue to think about this, it ultimately becomes clear that extreme caution should be used when we tax our most wealthy individuals or our businesses since they are the source of the vast majority of our jobs.

In fact, there is really only one valid reason to tax them at all. Simply stated, that reason is to ensure that the financial power of these individuals and businesses is never allowed to grow unchecked.

Clearly, we do not want to eliminate either the wealthy families or the large corporations. Many of us would like to be able to achieve that kind of economic status for ourselves and our own families. Thus, as a nation, we must always leave open to our self-employed individuals and small businesses the chance to get started and grow, just as today's wealthiest families and giant firms did in their earliest beginnings.

As a nation, we should always ensure that opportunity for another critical reason. Many fields of commerce could never even exist unless there were firms with tremendous financial resources to enter them. Denying them in this country would only mean that firms from other nations would become (by our own default) the dominant ones in these industries. Examples include railroads, steel manufacturing, chemical research and

production, pharmaceuticals, plus many more industries vital to our nation's strength and viability.

Finally, we can all recognize that these kinds of big-
ger organizations are often the ones most responsible
for making huge numbers of useful and desirable products and services available to us as consumers in such
wide fashion and at lowered prices.

*So while realizing the great benefit of having these
wealthy individuals and very large firms in our country,
we also see the strong need to always ensure that the enormous financial power that comes with their accumulated
wealth, income, and size does not exclude opportunities for
the small businessperson or enterprise.*

Once again, this is an important area where our
current system of taxes does not level the playing field
nearly as well as it should.

It is almost ironic that the changes needed to do so
require that our wealthiest individuals and largest corporations should pay based on what is essentially the
way we assess personal taxes today. In short, we need to
tax such individuals and businesses on the highest portion of their revenues rather than their profits or lack of
profits. Like we do today with personal taxes, we should
employ a graduated tax rate that starts only after higher
levels of revenue are reached but then steadily increases
as the individuals and companies get ever larger and
more resourceful. For individuals and businesses just
getting started and at the low-income end of this scale,
we need no revenue-based taxes, just as we attempt to
do today for our citizens living on smaller incomes and
resources.

Evaluating any individual or business on their ability to generate a profit with their investments or operations will continue to be the appropriate and best measure for investors, financial people, and economists. *Taxing them on that basis simply leaves too many difficulties unaddressed when we try to assess a fair amount as their part for contributing to our government's revenue needs.*

Two examples show how these difficulties currently exist. First, it should always be remembered that with very few exceptions, wealthy individuals, businesses, and other organizations are primarily motivated to increase their total revenues or sales *whether their expenses are high or low.*

In propelling their endeavors toward this growth, *revenues are the essential ingredient.* For any successful individual or organization, costs and expenses (particularly when these are *deductible*) can be manipulated once an adequate level of incoming revenue is established.

For those with great wealth or incomes and for very large and powerful firms, tremendous amounts of expenses can be manipulated in just such a fashion. This does not mean that such a manipulated expense is not a true business cost. In fact, a super-inflated salary paid to a high-ranking officer in a firm may well be justified.

Certainly, that super-inflated salary is a true expense for the business, but if its real purpose is to keep that employee from being hired away by a smaller competitor who has far less resources, then allowing the larger firm to include all of that salary in its tax calculations (so that it then pays less in taxes) means that our system is not helping keep the playing field level. *In fact, assess-*

ing the large firm on its profits only causes the rest of us to pay in more taxes. At the same time, it is helping the large firm maintain its already sizable economic power over the smaller company.

Several years ago, many of us listened with interest and concern while our federal government held public inquiries into the case of a well-known bank officer after he and his wife flew on company expense to a New Year's bowl game. The bank officer maintained that this was a proper expense since it was valuable public relations for his corporation if he and his wife (who apparently was not an employee) appeared at the game and various social functions held in the distant city during the week's festivities.

The bank officer may or may not have correctly judged the true value to his company of that exposure at the bowl game city. Certainly the sizable costs of his and his wife's activities were most likely paid by the bank as business expenses and subsequently deducted on the firm's tax returns for that year. Assuming that was the case, fewer taxes were paid for that year by the bank. *In that instance, the rest of us either paid more taxes or watched anxiously as our governments—federal, state, and local—all went deeper into debt.*

The second example is the major difficulty that remains when we hear about foreign corporations' ability to pay little or no taxes to our nation while transferring enormous profits back to their home office and country. This can happen in large measure because we tax those companies on their *reported* profits rather than their revenues generated in our country. *This approach provides the opportunity to manipulate their expenses and transfer huge untaxed profits made in this country back to their homeland.*

The way they can do this is very simple. While our government officials are prone to decry it as unfair, the fact is these foreign businesses are only doing what all of us should do and what our present tax approach tells them to do—minimize the particular taxes owed by each of us.

When a subsidiary in this country purchases anything, they make as many of those transactions as possible with one of their parent firm's companies outside this country. And the prices they pay to those in their home country will be just as high as their revenues here permit. In this way, the parent company shows its tremendous profits elsewhere, while their subsidiary in the United States can report little or no profits—and minimal or no taxes—in this country.

Distributing Tax Revenues

Each type of governmental body requires two separate types of funding from us. Like our individual family budgets, they must have:

1. money for their various annual operations and capital projects.

2. savings or a reserve account needed for economic downturns or war.

Funds for their annual operating budgets are necessary for day-to-day operations of the various boards, commissions, agencies, and bureaus that virtually all governments must set up to do the things we want of them. These funds will be controlled, just as they are today, by our elected officials and those they appoint.

Funds for reserves are quite different, however, and our new tax approach must enforce this important fact!

Reserve accounts are necessary because of the one significant weakness in having our nation begin relying more on a National Sales Tax to pay for our governments. During times of economic downturn or war (when extra government expenditures are sometimes needed to reverse those conditions), sales tax collections slow down as each of us reduces the amounts and number of purchases we would otherwise be making. Thus, we must think of these federal, state, and local reserve accounts as our governments' savings for a rainy day.

Experts in the field of financial planning can tell us with a great deal of precision how much needs to be in these reserve accounts once our elected officials have established the appropriate criteria and goals. Similarly, experts in the field of economics can tell us when a downturn or recession has begun and when it is over. With these abilities in mind, our new tax plan will require that our elected officials accept a fiduciary responsibility to establish appropriate criteria and goals for these economic downturn and wartime reserve accounts, and to direct economically sound use of them when they are to be spent.

However, the actual amounts that *must* be kept in these various reserves will be determined *only* by independent panels of financial planning experts. In the case of reversing economic downturns, the release of these funds will be allowed *only during times determined not by our politicians but by an independent panel of economic experts*. For the other reserve, a formal declaration of war by Congress will automatically release those federal funds.

Another very important consideration that must be dealt with concerns which type of government should receive the tax dollars collected.

The types of governments who should receive our taxes are:

- Federal government
- State governments (including state toll highway commissions and other similar statewide authorities)
- County, city, town, village, and other similar local government bodies having elected officials.

Which government body receives how much should depend on which jobs we expect of each. It should be very important that each service we wish to be done by any government body be assigned to the most local level possible. This way will place it under the responsibility of elected and appointed officials closest to individual voting electorates.

National defense and the promotion of strong commerce for the country should be the primary jobs of our United States or federal government. Most functions currently performed by the departments of defense, state, justice and treasury should continue essentially as they now exist.

Present state governments should continue much as they do today, including their divisions—such as counties or parishes. They should also be the ones specifically charged with meeting the needs in our poorer rural areas.

County, city, town, and village governments should continue essentially like they do now, except that their roles in helping to meet the needs of our urban-poor neighborhoods should be increased[9] in proportion to the decreased role now normally attempted by federal bureaucracies.

With these jobs and primary functions, it becomes possible to see better how our taxes should be distributed.

Type of Tax or Dues	Government Recipient
National Sales Tax	(a) Amount equal to the year's federal budget to the United States.
	(b) Two percent (for urban-poor needs) to counties, cities, towns, and villages.
	(c) Two percent (for rural needs) to participating states.
	(d) Remaining balance to states and from there to counties, cities, towns, and villages divided as:
	(1) Forty percent based on the location where the taxes were collected.
	(2) Sixty percent based on population.

---

9 This does *not* mean that existing welfare programs should be continued. Instead, it should allow each locale to establish and maintain those programs its citizens accept as needed for their community.

All sales tax amounts distributed will be designated for use in meeting the particular government body's operating budget. Once any jurisdiction's budget estimate for that year is met, all remaining dollars for that governmental body will be used first to complete funding any reserve requirements. Finally, one-half should be used to reduce any debt principle owed by that electorate, and the other one-half or otherwise remaining amounts will then be deposited in an escrow account of the United States for refund to the particular jurisdiction's *citizen* taxpayers early in the following year.

High Revenue Taxes   (a) Fifty percent to the United States and from there equally divided between the economic and wartime reserves.

(b) Fifty percent to participating states and from there to counties, cities, towns, and villages divided as:

(1) Forty percent based on the location where the taxes were collected.

(2) Sixty percent based on population.

All High Revenue Tax amounts distributed will be designated for the receiving government's reserve accounts. Once any jurisdiction's reserve requirement is fully funded, one-half of all remaining dollars will be used to pay any of that jurisdiction's debt principle, and the other one-half or otherwise remaining amount refunded to its *citizen* taxpayers.

National Dues Payments (a) One hundred percent to the United States.

All National Dues payment amounts will be designated for equal division between the federal government's reserve accounts.

National Dues Refunds (a) One hundred percent from the United States.

All National Dues refund amounts will be paid from the federal government's economic downturn reserve fund and only to citizens of participating states and local governments.

The two special distributions of the National Sales Tax collections will be set up to assist our urban-poor and rural population segments. These distributions will be available only to participating local and state government officials respectively. Their purposes will be to fund projects and other specially-designed efforts that can reasonably be expected to help these two groups of citizens. These funds will be strictly limited to the following population segments:

Urban-Poor Geographic Neighborhoods

- High population density, *and*
- low level of economic activity or average income.

Rural Geographic Areas

- Low population density, *and*
- low level of economic activity or average income.

Our local elected officials will compete for the first of these funds by submitting detailed proposals describing how and with whom they will be spent. Then these dollars will be distributed from the Urban-Poor account based on the merit and degree to which those proposals are likely to be met as decided by independent panels of experts equally divided from the fields of financial planning, economics, and community services planning. The *only* information to be used by these panels will be the official documents submitted by those local governments in which the proposed projects would be implemented and the performance record (from previous such grants) of each involved person, organization, and government body.

The same process will be used to distribute dollars from the Rural account to the various states. In this case, the independent panels would be made up of equally divided numbers of experts from the fields of financial planning, economics, and rural services planning.

Throughout this new approach to distributing the taxes and other dollars we pay for our various governmental bodies, two very important rules must be adhered to as tightly as possible.

These two rules are:

1. No distribution of taxes or other dollars will be based on or determined by the amount of any government body's budget estimates, except where this cannot be avoided. If such a calculation cannot be avoided, its effects on other jurisdictions must be absolutely minimized.

This rule is necessary to reduce the gamesmanship that officials who must set these budgets will otherwise be tempted to use in their deliberations and actions.

2. No tax or other dollars and no property having any value will be allowed to be kept by any state or local government organization when those funds and property result from any action by that entity or a closely aligned one.

This will go far to eliminate even the appearance that a government body might take any action toward passersby to increase their own income[10] or lengthen their existence beyond the actual need for such an organization.

Both are important because they will minimize the temptations that every elected and appointed official is bound to feel to make decisions or act in ways that can increase their jurisdiction's income from these taxes, levies, tolls, and fines. Instead, our new tax plan's goal is to have each budget of our various governments be set at its proper amount—not one penny more or less than is actually appropriate for and wanted by the particular electorate—and then adequately funded by those citizens and others living and visiting in that jurisdiction.

---

10 With this rule we will be able to see the rural sheriff's deputy stopping interstate highway traffic without the feeling that they are simply doing that to add revenue to their county's budget at the expense of others who live and vote elsewhere.

Types and Roles of Organizations

While the businesses and other legal organizations that operate within our nation today will not change, it is important to clarify the roles they perform in our society. Doing so very briefly now will help significantly to understand how they should play in our new tax approach.

The functions they perform are critical to our nation's (and therefore our individual and personal) well-being. In broad terms, there are four such functions that we must have to be a workable society that can provide each of us real chances for "life, liberty and the pursuit of happiness." These are:

- *Provide the goods and services we need and want*—Few of us would want to return to a time when we had to do everything for ourselves. When people had to provide their own food, build their own houses, weave and sew their own clothing, little or no time remained for the other activities of life that we now enjoy. Virtually no time or energy was left over to provide for financial and other forms of personal and family security.

- *Promote ideals, causes, and interests*—To be a workable society, we need more than things to fulfill our lives, our intellects, and our spirits. Thus, we must sometimes champion ideals (such as our religions), causes (such as finding a cure for a particular disease), and interests (such as trying to improve the public's understanding of the usefulness of an industry). Without this type of promoting, our intentions may be excellent, but our deeds simply would not get much real action started.

- *Provide charity to our less-fortunate neighbors*— No matter how much we want to believe that everyone is created equal, the fact is that a truly functioning society needs to provide the means for the more fortunate of us to help those with *permanent* handicaps plus others whose personal circumstances require some *temporary* assistance before they can recover.

- *Provide employment for individuals*—Whether we are the type who finds great satisfaction in our work or one who just wants to lounge around the beach every day, each of us requires some way to earn our living unless (or until) we finally have acquired enough financial resources to earn it for us.

Much of the present greatness of the United States today lies in the fact that we can and do shape our businesses and institutions in multiple ways to best accomplish their individual goals and functions. For example, a *business* can range from the smallest self-employed individual, proprietorship, or *LLC* or *S* corporation up to the largest of *C* corporations. Our trade associations can exist from the informal group of merchants in a downtown area up to a large and well-funded group such as the Teamsters Union or the American Medical Association. Our charity efforts start with an individual quietly helping another and proceed up to a highly-organized system such as the United Way.

These have no need to change! Through this kind of diversity and flexibility, we can and do accomplish fantastic amounts of work and productivity that meets so many different types of needs. For our new tax approach, we simply have to think about our organizations and institutions in the following groups and with the following roles:

	Businesses	Associations	Charities
• Provide goods and services	x		
• Promote ideals, causes, and interests		x	
• Provide charitable aid			x
• Provide employment	x	x	x

Once we begin to think of our organizations in this hierarchy, two requirements emerge that we must use to decide how any such effort is classified for our new tax approach. First, any activity within an individual organization or institution that involves sales of goods or services at anything more than a intermittent or de minimus level will cause that entity (or individual) to be classified as a business[11]. Thus, an organization such as the American Automobile Association, which sells insurance products, must be classified as a business rather than an association. Only by totally separating itself from such sales activities can any organization continue to be classified as an association or a charity.

---

11 Many of our government bodies today will also fit this category because of their activities such as selling sanitation services and electric power, charging fees for visits to state and national parks and other similar endeavors. Except for sales efforts that are clearly de minimus in scope and frequency, no real differences exist here from that of any business providing goods and services to its individual customers who can choose whether or not they want to buy.

Similarly, any organization or institution that espouses to even the smallest degree any ideal, cause, or interest and does not sell goods or services must be classified as an association. A church or sect that promotes a particular belief system, a chamber of commerce pushing for better business conditions, and an environmental group interested in stronger laws to protect wildlife would all fall into this classification.

Finally, while each and every individual and organization can (and hopefully does) act to promote and even donate assistance to others, only those entities that are not classified as either a business or an association can be a charity.

The second requirement that emerges when we think of our organizations in this hierarchy is that *virtually any charity provided by an individual, business, or association should be commended.* However, neither such charity nor the promotion of even the most universally-accepted ideals can continue to be a basis for changing that organization's classification in any way or to any degree.

It is also very important to realize that all of these types of organizations share one role in common—that of providing employment to us as individuals.

Important Details

Estimating An Individual's National Dues

While at first glance it may seem complicated, *this process is actually very simple and straightforward*—and it requires essentially nothing be provided to any government body. *Instead, it requires honest information be provided to us by our elected officials and all other public servants.*

First, by August 31 of every year each participating government body—federal, state, and local—will be required to set their operating budget amounts for the coming year. For any that do not meet this deadline, a level equal to 95 percent of their current year's appropriations will be automatically designated for them.

These budget amounts will be totaled and then divided by the number of citizens living within the particular jurisdiction[12], although children up to the age of two will not be counted, and children from two

---

12   The population figure to be used in this per capita calculation will be equal to the actual number of its citizens with National Dues filed for the preceding December 31. No politician's or bureaucrat's estimates will be used.

through the age of eighteen will be counted at the rate of 50 percent[13].

For example, a township with 5,000 people over eighteen, 1,200 young people between the ages of two and eighteen plus 200 very young people under two years of age will report a total of:

Persons over eighteen	5,000 x 1.0 = 5,000
Persons between two and eighteen	1,200 x 0.5 = 600
Persons under two	200 x 0.0 = 0
Total Persons (for Dues)	5,600

Continuing the example, if this township's budget for the coming year is set by August 31 at $16,800,000.00, its portion of the National Dues of each of its residents would be that amount divided by 5,600, or $3,000.00 per capita.

Budgets, total persons (for dues), and per capita dues for the nation and each state and other local government will be set the same way as for the township.

By October 15 of the year in which the budget amounts are set, those who wish to can then calculate their or their family's estimated National Dues for the coming year. Using the per capita budgets published by the federal government at that time, they can simply add together the appropriate amounts for the nation, state, and city where they expect to reside during the coming year.

For example, if their state and national per capita dues will be $ 1,000.00 and $ 2,000.00 respectively,

---

13   For the purpose of determining each child's situation, their age on January 1 of the coming year will be used.

each adult citizen of the above township will estimate their coming year's National Dues as:

Township Per Capita Dues	$ 3,000.00
State Per Capita Dues	1,000.00
Federal Per Capita Dues	2,000.00
Total National Per Capita Dues	$ 6,000.00

A husband and wife in this township will each have estimated dues of $6,000.00, or a total of $12,000.00. A ten-year-old child in this family will have estimated dues of one-half each adult's amount, or $3,000.00, while a nine-month-old sibling's dues estimate will be $0.00 for the coming year.

Should the four people in this family plan to move to another state during the coming year, their estimates would change only slightly. If the published budgets for the new state's per capita dues were $1,400.00 and the new city's figure showed $3,400.00, then the amounts for the new residence will be $6,800.00 after adding in the unchanged national per capita dues amount.

Only their appropriate shares of each locale's amounts will apply for the year of their move. If this family expected to spend 50 percent of the coming year living in each of the two areas, their National Dues will be estimated for each adult as:

Old Township Per Capita Dues	$ 3,000.00 x 50 percent =	$ 1,500.00
New City Per Capita Dues	3,400.00 x 50 percent =	1,700.00
Old State Per Capita Dues	1,000.00 x 50 percent =	500.00
New State Per Capita Dues	1,400.00 x 50 percent =	700.00
Federal Per Capita Dues	2,000.00 x 100 percent =	2,000.00
New Total National Per Capita Dues		$ 6,400.00

Using these figures the family's new individual estimates[14] will now be:

Each Adult	$ 6,400.00
Ten-Year-Old Child	3,200.00
Nine-Month-Old Baby	0.00

In addition to the applications for children discussed above, two other special cases will also apply.

First, active duty members of our national defense service branches plus active participants in national alternative services designated by Congress (such as the Peace Corps) will be exempt from any National Dues, and United States citizens living in another country will be responsible only for the federal portion of their National Dues. However, these exemptions will apply only to those individuals and their immediate family members who reside with them.

Second, these National Dues will also apply to each part-time resident in the United States. Only tourists and members of the diplomatic corps from other countries will not be responsible for paying any National Dues. All other foreign citizens living in this nation, whether legally or illegally, will owe their share of National Dues (and High Revenue Taxes, if appropriate). They will be required to submit the same tax reports as each citizen, and they may claim any applicable credits to offset their individual or family's

---

14 Actual estimates would be done on a daily basis with each day accounting for 1/365th, or approximately 0.27 percent, of each year.

National Dues. However, they will *not* be entitled to any National Dues refunds.

All foreign nationals, except tourists and diplomats, will be allowed entry *only* after paying in advance or posting adequate security to cover their estimated dues. When they leave the country or at the end of any tax year, they can file their tax returns to claim any credits due them and to receive back any excess funds they were previously required to pay.

Foreign nationals who enter this country illegally will, upon detection, be required to pay their share of estimated dues plus a fine designed to assist in the recovery of the cost to our government agencies required to "police" such groups. Also, any individuals or businesses who employed them, whether knowingly or unknowingly, will be severely fined. They will also be responsible for the illegal immigrant's dues and fines should these turn out to be uncollectible from that foreign national. Finally, if either party is subsequently found guilty of more than one such instance or practice of this or a similar type, they will then be punished under federal criminal laws requiring prison sentences that cannot be shortened by any parole board.

Determining An Individual's Actual National Dues

Just as estimating one's National Dues turned out to be simple and straightforward, so too is the subsequent process of actually determining and reporting them.

In late December of the tax year and using the per capita dues amounts for each city and state plus the nation published in October of the previous year, the taxpayer's earlier estimates will be revised to simply include the actual number of days they resided in any particular locale. If the original estimates were exactly correct in predicting that person's actual places of residence, then the actual dues will precisely match the previous estimates.

Changes from their previously estimated dues will occur only if individuals moved their local residence more often or at different times from those estimated earlier. Using the example from the previous section but assuming that the adults and two children actually moved a month and a half later than originally estimated, the following shows their actual National Dues for that year:

Old Township Per Capita Dues
January 1 to August 15 (227 days) $ 3,000.00 x .6219 = $ 1,865.70

New City Per Capita Dues
August 16 to December 31 (138 days)   3,400.00 x .3781 = 1,285.54

Old State Per Capita Dues
January 1 to August 15   1,000.00 x .6219 = 621.90

New State Per Capita Dues
August 16 to December 31   1,400.00 x .3781 = 529.34

Federal Per Capita Dues
January 1 to December 31 (365 days)   2,000.00 x 1.0000 = 2,000.00

Total Actual National Dues $ 6,302.48

Using this calculation, the actual individual dues that the members of this family will report on their tax return will be:

Each Adult	$ 6,302.48
Ten-Year-Old Child	3,151.24
Nine-Month-Old Baby	0.00

Since there will not be a government requirement to have previously estimated one's National Dues except for foreign nationals planning to stay for longer periods, many citizens may not have made an earlier estimate. In such cases, this step will be the first time they make these calculations.

Determining an Individual's Actual National Dues Credit and Payment or Refund

Credits toward our individual National Dues in any given tax year will give each of us a real opportunity to eliminate having to actually pay that amount or any portion of it. For those of us with the least financial resources, they will even provide the chance to earn a refund payment[15].

Instead, our national government and each state and local government will receive the vast majority of

---

15   This refund payment is more accurately defined as a payment (or reward) by the government for both taking care of our own and our family's needs *plus* the extra volunteer efforts which improved our national society and reduced the need for additional public spending. Since no actual payment will have been made toward any citizen's National Dues, no actual refund can apply. However, to this writer the word *refund* seems to convey the concept better than does the word *payment*.

their necessary tax funding through the National Sales Tax each of us pays as the year progresses and the High Revenue Taxes paid by the wealthiest individuals and organizations in our country.

Two types of credits will exist. The first of these will be those that reduce our individual or family dues and can actually result in a refund early in the following year. The second type of credits will also allow each taxpayer to reduce or eliminate a requirement to actually have to pay their National Dues amount *but cannot be used to generate a refund.*

Credits that can both reduce one's National Dues and go beyond that to generate a refund will recognize basic living necessities. They will also reward any adult's volunteer efforts that help make our society better and encourage our children to do their best in school.

Because of lifestyle differences, these basic living type credits—while equally applicable to all of us—will benefit most individuals and families with lower incomes. They will even allow the poorest of our fellow citizens to gain some partial refund through their volunteer work and thus effectively create some payment to them for their laudable efforts. It will not accomplish this through welfare, as we attempt to do today. Instead, it will reward volunteer work.

Coincidentally, credits for volunteer work will provide to persons or families with lower incomes a valuable means to reduce their National Dues in a way that builds up the self-esteem of the volunteer. These credits will also go far toward better recognition of the marvelous contributions of so many of today's volunteers, whether they come from poor or wealthy circumstances. Today's too often unheralded housewife and "soccer mom" who devotes personal time and energy to a local blood drive and the temporarily unemployed person who gives time at a soup kitchen, will now be able to help their family's tax situation in a more tangible way than under our present tax codes.

Credits of the second type that can only be used to further reduce or eliminate an individual's dues will recognize savings and investments in ourselves and our nation. They will apply to such things as personal education, wages, and tips we pay to non-dependents, non-basic housing, investments for savings plus retirement, and some optional insurance coverage.

Because these types of credits will be more effective for taxpayers with middle or larger incomes and financial resources, they will be used most by those groups. For this reason, no refunds will be allowed to result from them. Instead, their purpose is to provide incentives for these middle and higher income individuals and families to invest in things that will provide jobs and security for larger numbers of fellow citizens.

To distinguish these two types of credits, the first group that can help generate a refund will be referred to as *Basic Living Credits*. Those that cannot result in a refund will be called *Nation-Building Credits*.

Basic Living Credits

The following items that make up any individual's costs for meeting their most basic needs are those things that we will be able to use to begin reducing any need to actually pay our own National Dues bill each year.

The actual amount of credit each of us will be allowed to use is shown in parenthesis as a percentage of our National Dues amount for that year. For example, if the percentage shown is 12 percent and the individual's National Dues for that year are $6,000.00, then the maximum credit that person can take for that time will be $720.00[16]. The actual credit that any one of us can claim will then be the total amount (including sales taxes paid)—up to the maximum percentage figure—of all receipts for our purchases of such items.

(a) *Basic groceries (12 percent)* will consist of those food items bought from the grocery store or other such businesses that are not subject to the National Sales Tax. This credit type will *not* include any purchases of prepared foods at restaurants, sandwich shops, hot dog stands, donut stores, and other similar establishments. No credits can result from items grown by an individual for their own or family's consumption.

(b) *Basic housing and utilities (20 percent)* will consist of rent and mortgage principal and interest payments plus insurance costs and condominium fees on an individual or family's primary residence. Also included will be electric, gas, water, sewer, and sanitation services plus one telephone line without any premium features. Service charges and deposits paid for these

---

16 For the family of four used in earlier examples, and now assuming their National Dues amount applicable in their case is $6,000.00 per adult, the family's total becomes $15,000.00. Thus their Basic Groceries credit allowed would be 12 percent, or $1,800.00.

basic utilities will also be useable for credits so long as records are maintained as proof of these payments.

Payments that will not be applicable will include any premium items, such as extra telephone lines and features, additional water services for yard or pool use only and cable television movies.

(c) *Basic clothing (5 percent)* will consist of all payments including associated sales taxes for virtually any wearable articles excluding items that are obviously *not* basic such as tuxedos, evening gowns, and other similar apparel articles.

(d) *Medical and dental care (20 percent)* will include all costs anyone incurs for health care services. Payments to doctors, dentists, nurses, hospitals, assisted living or nursing homes, and hospices that exceed any amounts paid by our insurance policies or company benefit plans will be useable for this credit. In addition, any medical and dental insurance premiums will be applicable as well as other associated costs like mileage, parking, and special equipment required for medical conditions.

(e) *Long-term care insurance (8 percent)* will include all premiums paid to insurance companies for long-term care coverage of the costs of assisted care or nursing home and private in-residence care. Also included will be premiums for disability income replacement during periods exceeding two years.

Long-term care payments not covered by insurance will not be included, since this credit is intended to be an incentive for individuals and families to provide for their own future care needs through insurance purchased over many years before it is actually required. However, many of these types of costs, which will be incurred by taxpayers without or with less-than-full coverage, will be included under other credits such as basic housing or basic medical and dental care. For this reason, nursing homes and other care providers will be required to break down their charges into these categories.

(f) *Unemployment and disability insurance (8 percent)* will include all premiums paid to insurance companies for replacement of lost income during periods of up to two years.

(g) *Retirement plans (10 percent)* will include all payments into designated retirement investment plans, such as today's Individual Retirement Accounts (IRA), Keogh and 401(k) arrangements where significant restrictions exist against premature withdrawals. Contributions by an employer will not be available to an individual under this credit type, even though they will be permissible and encouraged.

(h) *Dependent care (7 percent)* will include all payments made to businesses or adult individuals (not including spouses) that provide services such as child daycare and eldercare to any person or family who *must* have this to work for income or for Volunteer Work Incentives credits.

Baby-sitting needed for recreational and other such activities will *not* be applicable for this type of credit. Similarly, summer camp activities for young family members will *not* be applicable, except where required for all parents or guardian family members to work for income or for Volunteer Work Incentives credits. In such cases, the camp's charges must be broken down to show which amounts paid were for overnight housing, food, medical care, and other types of services so the family can include them to the extent applicable only under those credit categories.

(i) *Volunteer work incentives and school participation (25 percent)* will include a credit equal to the number of hours of an adult's volunteer effort under the supervision of any officially-designated charity organization multiplied by $5.00. In a similar fashion, like credits will be applicable for volunteer work done under the supervision of officially designated associations where the individual's efforts are useful in improving our nation's environment. An example of this type of volunteer work includes picking up litter from a city park or various vacant lots.

Because of the potential for misuse, children may not earn any voluntary work credits. However, each young person from the fourth through the twelfth grades will be able to assist their family by staying in a bona fide public or private school (including a satisfactory attendance record of at least 95 percent). When this attendance record is met, those children may each then earn for their family an annual credit of $50.00 plus an additional $100.00 multiplied by their core curriculum grade point average[17] achieved for the academic year completed during the tax year.

---

17 Grading for these purposes will require the school to meet reasonable standards established every fifth year by an independent panel of experts from business and science; and will be based on a 4.0 scale.

For example, a taxpayer who donates sixty hours each year to the National Kidney Foundation plus sixty hours to an officially designated soup kitchen organization will be able to claim a credit of 120 times $5.00, or no less than $600.00[18] toward their own or their family's National Dues for that year, while their fourth grade child who earned a 3.2 grade point average will contribute an extra $370.00 for their completed school year.

In each tax year, Volunteer Work Incentives and School Participation credits earned by individuals and family members will be useful in two ways. First, where less than 90 percent of the individual or family's National Dues amount has been satisfied through the other Basic Living credit categories, they may be added to any Nation-Building credits to complete up to 100 percent of that obligation with no refund. Second, where the full 90 percent of their National Dues obligation has been met through the other Basic Living credit categories, Volunteer Work Incentives and School Participation amounts may be used to further reduce any National Dues obligations. Then, citizens may use these credits to earn a refund of up to 15 percent of the individual's (or family's) National Dues amount for the preceding year.

---

18   This amount will be significantly increased as an individual's volunteer hours grow. For example, in any month where one's volunteer hours exceed 10, their total time will be doubled.

No Volunteer Work Incentives credits will ever be applicable for any efforts done under the supervision or sponsorship of a government body. Even though these efforts normally will be just as commendable, this prohibition is absolutely necessary to ensure that our elected and appointed officials cannot use these tax credits in partisan situations.

Only volunteer work under the supervision of charities and associations that have been designated (after having met strict and high standards regarding such criteria as the percent of funds which actually reach their intended beneficiaries) will be eligible for this type of credit. Volunteer work done under other charities, associations, businesses, governments and even personal assistance, while extremely laudable, will not be useable for this credit.

Finally, even charities and associations that have been designated will have to be continually recertified at least once each year by an independent panel of experts from business management. The purpose of this is to ensure that they continue to meet the required standards.

Nation-Building Credits

These credits will consist of items that strengthen the United States and build its economy primarily through investments in its people and jobs creation. They will encourage each of us to save more and thus increase our personal wealth. Then we and our families can enjoy it during our lifetimes, and pass it on to our heirs in the ways we see as best.

Since this second type of credits will be of greatest attraction to middle- and upper-income taxpayers, they will be available only to further reduce or eliminate any remaining amount still owed on a given year's National Dues. Nation-building credits can *never* be used to produce a refund payment.

The actual amount of credit each of us can use from these categories is shown in parenthesis and is in addition to any dollars used for the year's similar or corresponding Basic Living categories. Because no refunds can be generated using these Nation-Building credits, percentages of the particular year's dues are no longer needed.

(j) *Other housing and utilities ($5,000.00)* will consist of rent, mortgage principal and interest payments plus insurance costs on an individual or family's primary residence that exceed those used for their Basic Living credits. It may also include any additional residences such as a vacation house, and these various residences may be combined up to the maximum limit of this credit type.

Rent payments plus any amounts for accommodations that are used as less-than-fulltime residential purposes will not be available for this credit except in short-term limited cases such as an emergency or job relocation.

(k) *Wages and tips paid to non-dependents (unlimited)* will consist of any payments made within the United States to non-family members for domestic help, restaurant service, airport skycap assistance, and other such forms of work. However, such payments will *not* be useable for this type credit if the payee is an illegal alien in this country.

(l) *Personal education ($2,000.00)* will consist of any payments for tuition, necessary textbooks, and materials plus other such items directly required because of attendance at any certified institution of learning. This will include preschools, primary and secondary public and private schools, technical and art institutes, plus colleges and universities within the United States. Similar institutions outside this country will *not* be included, except for United States citizens residing in a foreign nation *and* where the schooling is local to their place of residence.

The maximum amount of credit that can be used in any year will be limited to a relatively small amount to encourage individuals and families to *invest* their dollars in education funds well before schooling actually begins. Thus payments to educational accounts that are similar to today's Individual Retirement Accounts could be used for this credit. However, for those who do not utilize such educational accounts, any additional funds paid in such years will be able to be *carried forward* and used to reduce a subsequent year's National Dues.

In cases where previously invested funds are not needed for someone's education, and after that individual reaches the age of thirty years, those accounts may be transferred into a retirement account for that individual or another member of the immediate family.

(m) *Retirement investments ($5,000.00)* will consist of additional payments into designated retirement accounts such as a 401(k) or an IRA that are over and above those used for Basic Living credits.

(n) *Other United States investments ($2,000.00)* will consist of all payments and deposits (less comparable withdrawals) in savings accounts, mutual funds, domestic stocks, and bonds plus other similar domestic investment instruments. Also included will be net payments into most personal investments, such as an individual business enterprise or real estate to be used as rental property within one year of purchase.

Payments into such savings accounts and instruments, when made directly into foreign nations or institutions will be excluded. However, foreign investments such as stocks, bonds, or international mutual funds will be acceptable when made through a United States company[19].

(o) *Other medical and dental insurance ($1,000.00)* will consist of any premiums paid which exceed those used for Basic Living credits.

(p) *Other long-term care insurance ($1,000.00)* will consist of any premiums paid which exceed those used for Basic Living credits.

Determining a Year's National Sales Tax Percentage

The actual percentage for our National Sales Tax will have to be set in advance of each year at a level estimated to produce the revenues needed by the budgets

---

19 This would not apply for a company headquartered in the United States whose ultimate ownership is not in this nation.

of the various government operations. Thus, for each approaching calendar year, a new sales tax percentage statistically estimated by the Congressional Budget Office as necessary to meet the next year's federal operating budget plus the individual operating budgets for the upcoming year of all but the highest two of the states and highest 5 percent of all local government bodies.[20] This percentage level must then be certified at the next higher multiple of 0.10 percent and published by Congress no later than November 30 before it becomes effective on the following January 1.

Sales taxes will apply to most goods and services sold throughout the United States to any final consumer including individuals, businesses, associations, charities, and even governments. They will include services for real estate sales (such as appraisal fees) and *all* goods and services sold for use in foreign countries.

Except for sales to users outside this country, these taxes will not apply like any so-called value-added charge

---

20   This procedure—which seems much more complicated than it is in actuality—is necessary because the many budgets throughout the nation will not be individually met by a *single* nationwide percentage figure. Instead, the percentage determined will first fully fund the federal budget plus the urban-poor and the rural amounts. Then, it will also fully fund a theoretical level where each state will be assumed to have a per capita budget equal to that one with the third highest level among all participating states and each participating local government will be assumed to have a per capita budget equal to the one which ranks at the 95th percentile position among that group. Citizens of states and local governments with lower budgets will benefit through refunds in the following year.

to goods purchased for resale or as material to be used in a subsequent manufacturing or assembly process. Also, they will not apply to specific goods and services that are either basic living needs or to the sales price of land and buildings. Examples of excluded items will be very limited but will include rents and mortgage payments, insurance payments, educational expenses, investment purchases, and dependent care such as child and elder daycare. Additional examples include essential medical and dental products and services, assisted living and nursing home care, plus initial quantities of any utility services needed for basic living needs[21].

Purchases of food or grocery items will not be subject to any sales taxes, except where they are either nonessential or luxury items. Examples of taxable grocery items (which all stores must have clearly indicated on each label) will include snack foods, cakes and pies, most other bakery items (excepting basic types of breads), ice creams and yogurts, soft drinks and wines, premium cheeses, and any gourmet products. All prepared foods at restaurants, sandwich shops, and other similar establishments will be subject to the sales tax.

---

21 Nonessential medical and dental services will consist of such things as elective cosmetic surgery, although orthodontic procedures will not be subject to sales taxes. Initial quantities of utility services on a given month's bill will consist of deposits, charges for installation, monthly charges for one telephone line and instrument, and costs for an amount of usage—such as a reasonable number of kilowatt hours of electricity—needed for basic living requirements. This latter item will vary by season and climate conditions using criteria established by Congress.

Sales taxes also will not apply to sales between persons not normally in the business of the particular transaction. For example, a purchase made at a neighborhood yard sale will not be subject to sales taxes, but similar items bought at a commercial flea market or from a street-side sandwich vendor will require that they be paid to the seller.

Barter situations between two individuals not normally engaged in that business will *not* be taxable. However, if one of the parties is sometimes in a related type of endeavor *or* incorporated, the transaction will be taxable.

At first, these sales taxes will be set at seemingly high percentages compared to our current levels, but they will be an equal percentage rate throughout the nation with only two limited—but significant—exceptions. They will apply to much lower prices, making their amounts far below those we would expect based on prices at this time[22].

The equal percentage rate throughout the country will have two very important advantages to many of us. First, it will virtually eliminate the hidden and surprise nature of many of today's unexpectedly large

---

22   Initially we might hear of a sales tax rate as high as 75 percent, and our thinking would likely suggest to us an extraordinarily high tax of $7.50 on an item we are used to buying for $10.00. But, in fact, the new tax rate will apply to a much lower new price—say $6.00, making the new total purchase $6.00 + $4.50, or $10.50—about the same, or even less, than we are currently used to paying when today's sales tax rate is added.

assessments that cities and states often use to ambush us when we stay at their hotels and motels or travel through their airports. These much-larger-than-normal sales tax add-ons all depend on the fact that as visitors we cannot easily learn about them beforehand. Thus, we are simply trapped by them when we go to check out of our hotel or pay for other services where there is no good alternative at the moment that we first become aware of these high taxes.

Second, the equal but higher sales tax rate will force buyers and sellers alike to acknowledge that the *real* price of any item about to be purchased includes *both* the seller's price *and* the sales tax. The importance of this is that *each of us will be far more aware of the actual cost when we consider buying a product or service.* This will help greatly to make us better consumers than today's approach where we are told the price is $99.95, when in reality it is normally anywhere from $104.95 to $114.95 (or even higher) after sales taxes are added.

These new sales taxes will be set at a specific percentage of the seller's price instead of being based on *tables*, as they are commonly done today. This will eliminate the misleading practice of states and cities that presently hope we will believe that a 5 percent table produces a 5 percent tax. In fact, these tables normally result in a *higher* tax rate than we are told.

The first of two limited exceptions to the equal percentage rate sales tax will apply only to a few consumer products and services that can be reasonably expected to create higher than normal costs or risks to individuals and therefore our nation. These few products and services will be taxed at a higher multiple of the year's nationwide tax rate to produce greater tax revenues that will help pay any additional cost their use will likely cause. These higher multiples of two, three, or more will be established by Congress every fifth year, as will the goods and services to which they will apply. The list might include items such as alcohol and tobacco products, skydiving equipment, or bungee-cord jumping services that could endanger our citizens' or visitors' health and well-being. Finally, should Congress consider it appropriate, this list may include such things as exotic television and movie releases, adult entertainment clubs, and explicit recording industry products that are felt by many to be injurious to our children.

The second of the limited exceptions to the equal percentage sales tax will allow a local government to establish optional percentages of no more (and no less) than 10 percent to be applied exclusively within their own boundaries. Such an option will permit a city or county on occasion to undertake large, short-term projects such as a new courthouse that is best financed separately and quickly.

These local optional amounts will never be allowed to last more or less than two years before they automatically expire unless specifically renewed by their appropriate local electorate. Also, they will be specifically prohibited from being applied on companies or individuals for sales made outside their jurisdiction (such as mail orders placed from their area to a catalog firm in another locality). Finally, no such optional sales taxes paid by any individual will be allowed to reduce in any way that person's or their family's National Dues.

The very stringent limitations on these optional local sales taxes are extremely important.

The amounts of "no more or less than 10 percent" will mean that local governments cannot simply add on small, less obtrusive tax rates (such as 1 percent) that might be approved by the local electorate more easily. They cannot implement large percentages for even the shortest period, such as when a major convention is in town for a week. Finally, the limited time periods of no more than two years also means that these optional add-ons will automatically expire unless the particular voters actually approve their renewal.

Prohibiting the collection of such optional add-on sales taxes on sales outside the area's boundaries will accomplish two critical requirements. First, it will prevent unwarranted intrusion by a local government into the activities of buyers and sellers in other areas. Otherwise, a situation would be created which amounts to taxation without representation.

Second, it will deny locales who will otherwise be tempted to put too much reliance on these extra revenues the ability to remain as attractive to both businesses and consumers as a place to live and work. Any local government that uses this option too often will find that tourists, business travelers, and even residents will realize that visiting, doing business, and living in that area will cost them much more over the long term. Such unfavorable comparisons with other areas will ultimately work to the disadvantage of those who overuse the optional sales tax provision.

By not allowing individuals to use any optional sales taxes they pay to reduce their National Dues, such local revenue-raising decisions will be prevented from adversely affecting taxpayers in other parts of the nation.

Adjusting National Sales Tax Percentages

Because of the very high operating cost we currently pay for our various government bodies, plus the extreme amount of public debt and its high interest cost, a new National Sales Tax plan will almost certainly have to begin with what will seem to be a very high percentage. *Fortunately, the prices that our businesses charge for the goods and services we need and want will no longer need to be as high as today's levels.*

This can be made to happen even faster. As consumers, we can do this by shopping only with businesses that actually reduce their prices in line with their lower costs.

In any event, the actual percentage for our National Sales Tax will have to be reset for each upcoming calendar year at a new level estimated to produce the revenues needed by the new budgets of the various government operations. The procedure for each approaching calendar year will be the same as described earlier and will be certified and published by November 30. Then on the following January 1, this new and hopefully lower sales tax rate will go into effect for the next twelve months.

For any given year in which the National Sales Tax percentage produces federal revenues that exceed the total of that government's operating budgets (including the Urban-Poor and the Rural amounts), this excess will be transferred to the reserve accounts for the federal government. Then, if those reserve accounts meet their required levels, one-half of any excess amount will be used to pay federal debt principle, and *a national per capita refund of the other half will be sent to each individual or family who filed a National Dues tax return for that year.* This refund—for United States citizens only—will be issued on July 4 of the following year.

Even before this occurs, most individual states and local governments will normally find that the National Sales Tax produces revenues that exceed their budgets, especially when their operations are well run and no unusual emergencies occurred. When this is the case, all excess sales tax collections that would otherwise be due to their operating budget account will instead be sent to that jurisdiction's reserve account. Finally, if their reserve account becomes fully funded as a result, one-half of all remaining excess revenues will be used to reduce their debt, and the other half will provide refunds to that jurisdiction's citizens on a per capita basis on April 15 of the following year.

For any government body—federal, state, or local—able through good management to operate at less than their established budget for a given year when the National Sales Tax produces sufficient revenues, any excess (up to the budget level) will also be refunded to that jurisdiction's citizens on a per capita basis on April 15 of the following year.

The great importance of this yearly process cannot be stressed too much. By adjusting our National Sales

Tax rates this often and so close to the actual budget years, voters will be far better able to ensure that our government officials respond to the various electorate's desires. The same will also be true of the use of refunds earned before great lengths of time have elapsed in the following year. We cannot allow these acts to be delayed by our politicians and their appointees and then find the funds diverted to other political uses.

By making these adjustments and refunds so soon after any given year's actual government expenditures, it will be far more likely that our officials will become more responsible with their budgets—and our money.

Collecting National Sales Taxes

Only at those times when we individually choose to purchase the goods and services we need or want will sales taxes be collected from us or our family members.

National sales taxes will be collected at the time of a sale (or in the case of rental and lease type arrangements as an appropriate portion of each regular payment) by the business or the self-employed individual who is the seller. Then they will be turned over to the federal government's agency (the Internal Revenue Service or its successor under our new tax approach) within no more than the next month.

This is exactly the way sales taxes are collected and handled in most cases today, except that they are normally remitted to the various state tax departments.

Also, as is the case today, each self-employed person and business will be paid a very small but important commission, starting at 2 percent of the amounts collected to cover their costs of acting as one of the nation's tax collectors. For those businesses that will be collecting very large amounts, these commissions will be capped at a reasonable amount (say $500.00) per month. The essential idea here is to ensure that the government receives our tax dollars promptly, while the businesses are paid for at least some of their cost of collecting these funds and the associated paperwork.

Once the federal tax agency receives these funds, it will *immediately* forward to each state and local government their share for use as budgeted by those locally elected officials.

Three extremely important goals are accomplished with this approach. These are:

1. Our government's costs for collecting taxes will be dramatically reduced

2. These funds will begin flowing to our federal, state, and local tax agencies *almost immediately* and will continue with each passing month so that withholdings will no longer be required from our paychecks and other transactions.

3. No government agency has any need to know who of us paid or how much.

Since significant portions of all sales taxes collected will go back to the state and local governments, it will be necessary that the businesses that collect them identify the local area where they were paid. This will allow these tax payments to be sent back to the taxpayer's local area or better divided between those areas where that individual's time is spent.

As an example, most of the sales taxes paid by a retired couple (who live in one place but spend two months of each year traveling elsewhere in this country), will go back to their home state and city. However, the amounts paid by them while at other locales will be better apportioned among the cities and states they visited.

Only two exceptions will apply to the requirement for our businesses to identify the local area.

First, businesses that often sell at locations other than their own (such as mail order-type operations) will have to divide the taxes they collect so that the various locales of the buyers can be reported. In this way, taxes collected by them will be returned ultimately to the purchaser's state and local government rather than the area where the firm's headquarters is located. Similarly, businesses with multiple stores will have to report tax collections by each outlet's locale.

By requiring this first exception, our new tax approach will be able to divide the funds received in a far better fashion between the various government bodies and jurisdictions where we each spend time and enjoy their services. At the same time, those cities—where operations such as the large mail-order firm are located or with major manufacturing corporations (who collect no sales taxes)—still enjoy the significant advantages those firms provide in the form of extra employment for their area's citizens.

The second exception involves purchases made while visiting a foreign country or through an operation, such as a mail order firm located outside this nation's borders. In these cases, the amount of sales tax will be based on the actual price converted to our dollars or the most comparable domestic price of equivalent items, whichever is higher. These taxes will be collected by customs offices at the port of entry into this country or by the domestic shipping company at the time of delivery. These collections will not be identified with any specific locale but will be put into the pool of all other sales taxes for ultimate distribution to our federal, state, and local governments.

Sales taxes collected by firms and self-employed individuals will not be part of their business revenues. Therefore, shortfalls in collections, late collections, or any other such difficulties between them and the federal tax collection agency to which they must send these funds will be their responsibility. Their individual customers—who were the taxpayers at the time of a purchase—will not be responsible in any way, except where it can be clearly established that the buyer was properly informed but failed to pay the appropriate sales taxes to the seller. An example where the buyer will be responsible would be payment by a check that is subsequently and properly dishonored for insufficient funds, while an inappropriately dishonored check will shift responsibility to their bank.

Because sales taxes collected will not be part of the revenues of any seller, they will not be considered part of their assets should that person or firm become insolvent or otherwise go out of business. Thus, should proceedings such as a bankruptcy occur, any sales taxes that had been collected but not yet paid to the government will be paid first and at 100 percent value before any other debts.

Finally, any unpaid tax collections that might remain after all remedies have been exhausted will become the personal and proportionate responsibility of the owners (such as parent organizations) or shareholders. Should they fail to finally pay their share within two years of official notification, criminal penalties will be applied. In the case of corporations, these criminal penalties will be assessed to all appropriate top officers and directors under laws that assume any guilt resides at the highest levels (in descending order of rank), unless it can be shown clearly that lower ranking officials were responsible and were not acting under any duress from their superiors in the business.

High Revenue Taxes

Like all of us, organizations will pay sales taxes on goods and services they purchase for their own use. But unlike the rest of us, no organization should pay or be accountable for any National Dues. Instead, their payment for the privilege of being able to operate within this marvelous nation will be made in two other ways. These are:

1. Businesses provide each of us with those goods and services that we as individuals and families need or want, and in so doing, they also furnish the nation a very powerful engine, or driving force for our economy. Associations and charities provide each of us with the additional things we need and want to make our society and living conditions better. They give us leadership and inspiration; plus they provide many

ways through which each of us can contribute to a more civilized and beautiful country.

2. Businesses, associations, and charities *all* provide individuals with employment that in turn enables us to build personal and family wealth.

Considering how important these two contributions are to each of us, *only one reason can remain for taxing organizations*. This reason also applies equally to our nation's most wealthy and highest income individuals because once they have achieved such status, their motives and actions can and normally do become very much like those of organizations.

As organizations and individuals grow larger in their ability to generate revenues, they also become more and more powerful and economically efficient. Whether or not they misuse this power and efficiency, they will always be tempted to do so in ways that can negatively affect the rest of us as individuals and our much smaller businesses who are just getting started or are simply struggling to survive in a competitive marketplace.

Thus, the only way to keep available to our nation a means for smaller firms and self-employed individuals to start-up their dreams and ideas or survive among the giants is to continually do what we can to level the playing field between the powerful and the little guys.

One way this can be aided is to reduce the power of the wealthy and those larger organizations with additional taxes that begin to apply only *after* their revenues reach much larger amounts. At that point, these taxes should begin small and then grow steadily as the revenues of these organizations, individuals, and families increase up to the very largest levels.

At the same time, *we should also do everything possible to keep this step from becoming nothing but a penalty on their successful accomplishments!*

To do this we should allow them some good *options* for reducing their otherwise continually increasing tax rates. With such options, they could then decide for themselves whether they want to let the government spend their dollars *or if they want to personally direct those dollars to the nation's needs about which they feel most strongly.* These options should work in areas of the nation's most critical needs including jobs creation, domestic investments, greater educational opportunities for citizens and charity.

The point here is essentially two-fold. First, they can supply their extra dollars to government officials who will decide where to spend them—likely with less effectiveness and potentially with some graft. *Or they can use those funds in ways they believe more efficient and worthwhile.* Second, if their extra dollars are used in more effective ways, then *the High Revenue Tax really becomes more akin to good insurance by making the nation stronger and a better home for their wealth.*

There are even more very important reasons we do not want to deny any citizen or domestic organization the opportunity to achieve tremendous size!

1. *It will only defeat some of our nation's vital interests.* Giant firms and extremely wealthy individuals will always be a fact-of-life in other countries, and in many critical industries very large

endeavors are required *just to keep our nation in some areas of world competition* (such as an airplane manufacturing company).

2. As consumers we can appreciate very much the fact that these large operations can often offer both lower prices and many items that otherwise would never be available to us.

3. The wealth these individuals and organizations possess has to be a backstop for all of us in times of ultimate economic stress. We need look no further than our nation's founders who clearly recognized that whenever usual revenues sources were insufficient, they had to rely on the wealthy for either loans or gifts. *Surely, in our current economic climate we have learned that there are clear and practical limits on too much reliance in loans.*

Thus, we should want to "strike a good balance" between this and the very important need to always leave open the opportunity for much smaller businesses and individuals to start up and survive. Not only is it likely that many of us will personally wish to attempt such an endeavor, but we all sense the fact that such smaller efforts are frequently far more service-oriented and customer-friendly.

Traditionally, we have measured our organizations and self-employed individuals by their net profits, which are simply their total revenues minus their total costs. For accounting and economic evaluations, this should not change.

However, for determining their taxes, this traditional approach should and will change under our new approach to paying for our government.

There is a major reason this change is necessary. Our current approach simply allows the amount of taxes owed to be too easily manipulated by a large organization or wealthy individual. If the revenue coming in is greater than the costs that are *absolutely necessary*, an organization can simply overpay a top executive the difference. Or a foreign-owned manufacturer can increase the amounts it pays for parts from its parent's other subsidiaries in another country so that its real profits are transferred out of the United States.

When these kinds of manipulations reduce the amount of taxes owed, our government (and its taxpayers) end up paying the extra costs of the individual or organization doing these manipulations.

For example, if a large company expected to *break even* for the year but actually ends up with extra sales of $750,000.00, it can simply give its top executive those dollars as bonus perks such as a tax-free vacation. By doing so, it appears to have eliminated any profit—*and the tax that would have been owed* on that profit. If that tax would have been $250,000.00 to the various governmental bodies but now becomes zero because of the bonus, *our elected officials will have to get the $250,000.00 elsewhere—such as through higher taxes on the rest of us—or our public debt will go up.*

In this example, the top executive may or may not have deserved the bonus—and the decision to award those dollars is clearly one that only the company should make. But the reduction in taxes and the fact that *other taxpayers have to help make that payment* is not the best way for the nation.

A far better approach is to let the company make the decision it believes is correct when paying the top executive— but for our tax plan not to be affected by their decision.

To do this, we must change our tax approach. Thus, we will tax large organizations—domestic and foreign-owned—plus very wealthy and high-income individuals on the highest amounts of revenue[23] they receive in a given year. If they are in any way part of a larger organization or family—such as a subsidiary, joint venture, or other similar liaison arrangements— their tax rates will be determined by the consolidated or total revenues of all the involved parties.

It is vital that we apply these new tax rules equally to everyone, despite the fact that some will think that doing so is too drastic. Our new tax rules for large businesses and very wealthy and high-income individuals will also be required for the nation's large associations (including churches), big charities, and even individual government bodies that continue to receive great amounts of revenue from sources other than sales taxes and High Revenue Taxes. They will also be required of foreign firms and families residing in our country.

---

23 Revenues will include any money received except proceeds from issuing stocks or bonds, loans, insurance payments, re-funds of previously paid costs and sales taxes collected on customer's purchases. Interest, dividends, any extraordinary sales, kick-backs, or other payments by suppliers for such things as premium shelf displays in a retail store, lowered fees by banks, government grants and subsidies are all examples of revenues that will be subject to this High Revenue Tax.

This has to be the case if we are to create a reasonably level playing field for the entire nation.

Only three types of costs will be deductible.

The first of these exceptions will be that any endeavor may deduct its *domestic* purchases of raw materials and inventory. Farmers will be allowed to lower their total revenue figure by the amount paid for seeds and fertilizers, and manufacturers will be permitted to reduce annual sales numbers by the costs for raw materials used in their production processes. Retailers will be able to adjust total sales in their stores by the amounts paid to buy the inventory sold to their customers.

In a similar vein, any charity or bona fide church may deduct its *domestic* purchases of goods that it subsequently donates to individuals it has determined to be in need. However, no business or other association will be allowed this deduction.

Foreign organizations and individuals operating within this country will *not* be allowed any deductions for their raw materials or inventory costs, except where they can clearly show that such items were purchased from domestic suppliers. This will encourage them to buy more from domestic suppliers. Further our tax authorities simply are not able to audit the true source of supplies from outside the United States. Therefore, we could not effectively prevent the transfer of their United States profits to another nation as happens so frequently under our current tax system.

The second exception will allow any organization or individual to deduct their actual salary or wage costs paid to each employee who is a United States citizen plus 50 percent of any tuition and training costs actually paid for training by others not affiliated with or "related" to the employer. However, this will be subject to a maximum deduction of $70,000.00 per individual; plus for each individual who receives any other perks—such as use of a car, free or reduced-rate parking, paid time off for union activities, medical insurance, and reimbursement for business meals and entertainment that otherwise would have been a personal expense for that individual—this maximum deduction will be reduced by the full and actual value of all such privileges provided to them or paid on their behalf[24].

The third exception will allow any organization or individual to deduct any costs of contributions to bona fide churches and charities.

No organizations or individuals will be allowed to deduct any other costs they incur. The dollars they spend for supplies such as paper and pencils, computer software and hardware, automobiles, insurance, rent, utilities, advertising, and company luncheons will no longer be deductible.

High Revenue Taxes will be assessed on a graduated scale that grows in 1 percent increments (up to a maximum of 80 percent) in a manner similar to the illustrative tables following:[25]

---

24 "Perks" that will not reduce this maximum will be strictly limited to paid time off for voting, jury duty and military or National Guard duty plus business travel items such as motel and mileage reimbursements where the expense is clearly over and above that person's daily living costs.

25 The actual starting points, the size of each increment and the maximum tax rates will be set by an independent panel of experts equally divided from the fields of economics and government finance at least two months

High Revenue Tax Table
(Illustrative Examples)

Example 1:

For Organizations -
   (1) Taxes start at $ 300,000.01
   (2) Taxes step up to next percentage
      level every added $ 15,000.00

For Individuals -
   (1) Taxes start at $ 100,000.01
   (2) Taxes step up to next percentage
      level every added $ 5,000.00

Tax Rate	Total Organization Revenues		Total Individual Revenues	
0%	$ 0.00 -	$ 300,000.00	$ 0.00 -	$ 100,000.00
1%	300,000.01 -	315,000.00	100,000.01 -	105,000.00
2%	315,000.01 -	330,000.00	105,000.01 -	110,000.00
3%	330,000.01 -	345,000.00	110,000.01 -	115,000.00
4%	345,000.01 -	360,000.00	115,000.01 -	120,000.00
5%	360,000.01 -	375,000.00	120,000.01 -	125,000.00
6%	375,000.01 -	390,000.00	125,000.01 -	130,000.00
6% plus an added 1%	Each additional increment of $ 15,000.00 above $ 390,000.00		Each additional increment of $ 5,000.00 above $ 130,000.00	
80%	All additional revenue above $ 1,500,000.00		All additional revenue above $ 500,000.00	

Example 2:

For Organizations -
   (1) Taxes start at $ 1,000,000.01
   (2) Taxes step up to next percentage
      level every added $ 200,000.00

For Individuals -
   (1) Taxes start at $ 400,000.01
   (2) Taxes step up to next percentage
      level every added $ 75,000.00

Tax Rate	Total Organization Revenues		Total Individual Revenues	
0%	$ 0.00 -	$ 1,000,000.00	$ 0.00 -	$ 400,000.00
1%	1,000,000.01 -	1,200,000.00	400,000.01 -	475,000.00
2%	1,200,000.01 -	1,400,000.00	475,000.01 -	550,000.00
3%	1,400,000.01 -	1,600,000.00	550,000.01 -	625,000.00
4%	1,600,000.01 -	1,800,000.00	625,000.01 -	700,000.00
5%	1,800,000.01 -	2,000,000.00	700,000.01 -	775,000.00
6%	2,000,000.01 -	2,200,000.00	775,000.01 -	850,000.00
6% plus an added 1%	Each additional increment of $ 200,000.00 above $ 2,200,000.00		Each additional increment of $ 75,000.00 above $ 850,000.00	
80%	All additional revenue above $ 17,000,000.00		All additional revenue above $ 6,400,000.00	

prior to the beginning of our transition to the new tax approach. These values will be adjusted each succeeding year for inflation. And every third year or upon a formal Declaration of War by the Congress, they will be reset by a new independent panel of economics and government finance experts. *The criteria mandated for use by these experts will be to set these values at levels which best balance national security with the need to ensure that small businesses and individual endeavors are always able to start-up and operate on a level playing field.*

The actual marginal tax rate assessed will be determined by first adding the total of all consolidated revenues including revenues reported by related[26] businesses, proportionate shares of revenues received by subsidiaries and joint ventures. For domestic firms, any such revenues gained outside this nation will be reduced, however, by all legitimate taxes paid in those countries. Then that percentage will apply as the starting point on the High Revenue Tax table for the organization's or individual's actual domestic revenues.

Payments will be due monthly based on projections made during each period for the year in total in a manner similar to current estimated tax payments by individuals. Final tax forms and payment of any net due amounts will be required by March 15 of the following year.

---

26   In addition to those overt cases where different organizations are clearly and legally related (such as subsidiaries and joint-ventures), our new tax approach will include all covert situations, and tax law will presume a relationship. Thus, the Board of Directors of a firm may include a person who is a board member, officer or upper-management employee of any other non-parent or subsidiary business so long as it includes all revenues reported by that person's other firms and endeavors (excluding Associations and Charities) in determining its own High Revenue Tax percentage for each appropriate year. An Association will be subject to this same rule only when its roster includes more than one person from an outside organization (including its related parties), while Charities will not be required to follow this rule.

Distributing Tax Revenues to Federal, State, and Local Governments

Tax revenues under our new approach will consist of dollars from three primary sources. Some small amounts (by government standards) will also continue to come from miscellaneous sources such as fines paid to law enforcement agencies and courts, auctions of government surplus and assets seized from criminals, unclaimed tax refunds and bank accounts, entrance fees paid to the National Park Service when we visit these important areas, highway tolls paid to a state authority, and assessments paid to bodies such as the Environmental Protection Agency.

The three primary revenues sources will be:

1. National Sales Tax
2. High Revenue Tax
3. National Dues

Of these three sources, the first two will generate the vast majority of our government's income. The third source will likely be very small compared to the others, and in some years, it will possibly even be negative when refunds are greater than dues actually owed.

Distributing these revenues among the various federal, state, and local governmental bodies in an appropriate and effective manner will be critical! To do this, we first need to recognize the best general uses for each revenue source. This will determine where each dollar will be initially deposited.

There are two general uses that are:

1. The operating budgets of each federal, state, and local government body.

2. The reserve fund accounts of each federal, state, and local electorate.

Each source of revenue must be designated as to which use is its primary responsibility, and *only* in those years when it generates more than is required by that primary use, will its excess amounts be distributed to the other uses[27]. *We must not allow politicians and partisan considerations to determine or change this method of distribution.*

Using these designations, the actual dollars collected from each source of tax revenues will be distributed as follows:

(a) National Sales Taxes collected by local businesses and self-employed individuals will likely constitute the largest source of funds in the early years of our new tax approach. This will be desirable for all of us, since these dollars will come far more from those taxpayers and their families among us who can best afford to pay.

---

27 As an example, National Sales Tax revenues should go first to satisfy the operating budget requirements of our federal, state and local government bodies. Then, if collections actually exceed these required amounts, the excess should be temporarily held by the federal tax distribution agency for prompt distribution to the reserve accounts of our federal, state and local government bodies. Finally, if these reserve account requirements are fully met and an excess still exists, those funds should be retained in the federal reserve deposits for debt principle prepayment and per capita refunds to each citizen taxpayer.

The total of all National Sales Tax dollars collected will be sent to the federal tax collection agency, where they will immediately be separated into five parts. The first two of these parts will each equal approximately 2 percent[28] of the total National Sales Taxes collected and will be used for the special needs of our nation's urban-poor areas (in the case of the first 2 percent account) and of our rural areas (in the case of the second 2 percent account). These two funds will then be available only to local government bodies with urban-poor areas and to states with rural areas. They will subsequently be distributed only to those participating local and state governments whose applications and proposals have sufficient merit in the judgment of (and with approval from) rotating independent panels of experts each equally divided from the fields of economics, government finance, and public services planning.

The third of the five parts will belong to the federal government for its operating budget. This part will equal the total of the federal budget set during the preceding year because we must be certain that our nation's defense needs plus all approved efforts to promote legitimate commerce for our country are funded.

This is critical for at least three reasons. First, if we neglect our national defense,

---

28 Actually these will amount to 2/104ths of the National Sales Taxes collected.

the nation's very existence is put at risk, causing all our other programs and efforts to be jeopardized. Second, strong commercial activity will create more jobs, better incomes for individuals, and greater sales tax collections[29]. Third, this will go far to help avoid continued deficit spending at the federal level, where our elected and appointed officials are so removed from us as individual voters and thus less responsive to our concerns than are their counterparts at the state and local levels.

The fourth and fifth parts will come from the remainder of our National Sales Taxes collected for that year and will be divided between states (and our counties, cities, towns, and villages) in our new tax system. This will be done so that 60 percent of this remainder will be divided between the states in proportion to their populations, while the other 40 percent will be sent to these areas based on the location where the taxes were actually collected. *Such a formula will direct the vast majority of our sales tax dollars that go to state and local government operations back to the locales where we individually live, work, and play.*

---

29 We should all remember at that this point that this wonderful nation that gives each one so many opportunities actually began its economic life as a country primarily engaged in commerce and trade. And even when we see such activities sometimes carried to excess, we should never forget how much we owe to our system of capitalism.

Specifically, the fourth part will amount to 40 percent of the remaining sales tax collections and will be prorated back to each state. The percentages to be used will be those represented by the amounts actually collected by businesses in each state.

Then, within each state, the funds received will belong to that state *plus* its counties, cities, towns, and other local governments since *both* have jurisdiction over each dollar that was collected within the various locales' boundaries. Therefore, this portion will be divided between each county, city, and town in direct proportion to the percentage of all sales taxes collected within that state that were actually collected in each of these jurisdictions.

Once this is calculated, the final step will be to give the state its share from each county, city, and town's proration by using the ratio of the state's per capita dues for that year to the total of that figure plus the individual county, city, or town's 'per capita dues. The county, city, or town's share will be the remainder[30].

Finally, the fifth part—which will amount to 60 percent of the remaining National Sales Taxes collected for the year (after

---

30 In those cases where county budgets also provide services within cities, towns or villages, an additional separation (similar to that previously described between the state and its local governments) will also be needed. For simplicity it is not included above.

deducting the Urban-Poor, the Rural, and the federal budget)—will be prorated to the states plus the counties, cities, and towns in the same percentages as their populations. The actual calculations will be done exactly as for the fourth part, except that census results and percentages will be substituted for tax collection amounts by locale.

At any time during the distribution of the fourth and fifth parts a state or local government's budget becomes fully met by these sales taxes, all additional amounts otherwise due that jurisdiction will be paid into its reserve account. When this latter account is fully funded, one-half of any excess amounts resulting from National Sales Tax collections will be used to prepay that jurisdiction's debt principle, and the remaining one-half or otherwise available amount will be refunded on a per capita basis to that jurisdiction's taxpaying citizens on April 15 of the following year.

If at any time during this same process, a state or local government manages to complete its operations at a level *below their previously established operating budget*, and when its reduced budget is fully met by these sales taxes, all additional amounts resulting from these reductions will be separately identified for a per capita refund to that jurisdiction's taxpaying citizens on April 15 of the following year.

(b) High Revenue Taxes will likely provide the second largest source of funds initially but should grow over the years to levels comparable to National Sales Taxes.

The primary use of High Revenue Taxes will be to fund the various reserve accounts to be available to our federal government during wartime or to our federal, state, and local governments during economic downturns when sales tax collections decline. Providing funds for these reserves will not only help individuals during such periods but will also act as a kind of insurance for the larger businesses and wealthy sectors of our nation.

The total of all High Revenue Taxes collected in each year will be divided into two parts each amounting to 50 percent of these dollars. The first part will then belong to the federal government's reserve accounts (i.e., 25 percent for economic downturns and 25 percent for wartime needs).

The second of these two parts will belong to the various state and local government bodies and will be distributed using the same method and percentages as for the fourth and fifth parts of the sales tax revenues. However, once each state and local amount due is calculated, only the actual dollars needed for each jurisdiction's individual reserve account (up to the amount calculated[31] as due to that government body) will be distributed to that state, county, city, or town. In each instance

---

31   This calculation will always be done *before* any excess amounts from a jurisdiction's operating budgets are distributed to the state so that refunds due to any electorate are not pre-empted by their state.

where less than the calculated amount is needed, the difference will go instead to the federal government's reserve funds for wartimes and economic downturn periods.

(c) National Dues and National Dues Refunds will be the smallest source of funds by a great margin. In some years, they may even amount to a minus when refunds actually exceed payments[32].

National Dues collected will all go into the federal government's reserve for economic downturns, and all National Dues Refunds will be paid from this same account.

Additional sources of government income will seem very large to us as individuals but will actually be minor revenue producers in the totality of our nation's tax system. These will be distributed as follows:

(d) National Sales Taxes collected by mail-order businesses and by our federal customs agencies plus domestic shipping companies on purchases made in foreign countries will be included in the totals for that type of tax. However, their collectors will have to report them as coming from the area of our nation that includes

---

32 Such a situation can be desirable for the nation as a whole. When it occurs it will mean that individuals and families with limited incomes are achieving these refunds *and* that volunteer work within the country is being given by large numbers of citizens. It will also mean that those individuals and families with middle to high incomes have used their savings and investments in our nation to reduce the National Dues payments they would have otherwise owed.

the residence of the individual purchaser or the intended ultimate use by the organization who was the buyer. Then that data will be used (instead of the locale of the collector) for all calculations involved in properly distributing taxes within our country.

In a similar fashion, businesses in non-participating states and locales who sell to customers that reside in another state will have to collect the federal, state, and local National Sales Tax amount. Then they too will have to remit these as coming from the area of our nation that includes the residence of the individual purchaser or the intended ultimate use by the organization who was the buyer.

(e) National Sales Taxes collected by our federal customs agencies on sales to customers in foreign countries will also be included in that type of tax[33]. However, they will not be identified as having any state or local origin and therefore will not be part of any calculations affecting tax distributions within our nation.

(f) Miscellaneous revenues of all other types collected by *any* federal, state, and local government body or authority will go to the federal reserve funds, except for revenues currently received by legally-established state and local

---

33 A special case of this type must be noted here. Sales of items which would not be taxed in this country because they are sold by a manufacturer or distributor to later be sold and taxed at the retail level (e.g. a large piece of earth-moving equipment or a computer mainframe), must include a sales tax amount that is based on the Manufacturer's Suggested Retail Price in the United States.

organizational entities with strictly designated purposes such as the building and operation of a state toll highway authority. Their revenues will go instead to that state or local government's reserve fund.

Closely related to this will be the handling of *all* assets (including cash and non-cash resources) that any government body receives (by seizure or otherwise from such sources as criminals, liens on individual taxpayer's assets for unpaid obligations and unclaimed property recovered by Customs agencies). In all cases, these will be turned over to the federal government where they will be required to be sold at public auctions to our citizens and organizations or destroyed when to do less is deemed illegal or harmful to our national security.

Prices of Consumer Goods and Services Under Our New Tax Approach

It is impossible to predict with certainty how the current prices for consumer goods and services that each of us need or want to buy will be affected under our new tax approach. However, *the significant economic forces that determine them will work to keep them down to competitive and near-current levels. In addition, our transition plan will include a major component to ensure businesses from manufacturers to retailers cannot ignore those forces.*

Under our new tax approach, prices in almost all types of businesses will be under great pressure to fall to levels where they, plus the new National Sales Tax, will be very similar to today's prices plus current sales tax amounts.

Further, most of the current system's disadvantages for the consumer will no longer be in effect. Examples of these current disadvantages include:

1. The actual sales tax amount can vary significantly for the same item priced identically by different businesses. This variance can make a big difference in the total price we end up spending.

2. Mail-order prices are often too high today because their amounts generally do not require that firm to add sales taxes on items sold to out-of-state buyers.

3. A satellite television service may be overpriced because it does not have to charge a city's excessive franchise fees that must be applied on a competing cable system's bills.

Why the businesses' portion of new prices will fall is simple and straightforward when we think a little more about it.

Considering today's costs from government alone, they will see tremendously reduced overheads. Land and building or rent expenses will be much lower with property taxes no longer in effect. Payroll taxes for matching social security and Medicare and expenses such as unemployment payments to state and federal agencies plus workers' compensation insurance policies will no longer be required. Fees for state and local business licenses will no longer be in effect.

Today, as consumers we pay for all these kinds of government costs. But because they are in the businesses' prices, we forget where they came from. They are hidden because governments load them onto our businesses who must then pass them on when we buy things we want or need.

Our new tax system gives both consumers and taxpayers a great advantage here. It takes both necessary entities, government and businesses, and recognizes that both provide us, their customers, with goods and services. Then it separates their costs so we consumers can more easily decide how much of each we really require or want.

One of the most potent government cost reductions these businesses will experience will be the unbelievable amounts of time and wages now required just to prepare and file so many applications, reports, and returns. All of us know from our own experiences just how unreal dealing with government bodies can be—and for our businesses, it is simply multiplied many times over our personal situations.

Not including this last saving in time and wages, the taxes and other government-mandated insurance, fees, and licenses alone will reduce many businesses' overheads by an additional 10 percent to 15 percent (or more).

The good effects of our new tax approach will not stop at this level!

In addition to significant reductions in their governmental overhead costs, businesses from manufacturers to retailers that sell products will see other important cost changes. These other changes will contribute *even more* to further lowering prices for us as their customers.

When they purchase raw materials to be used in their manufacturing processes or goods to put on their store shelves, they will do so from suppliers who have lower costs (and therefore reduced prices) for those materials and goods.

The full effect of these changes will vary considerably from one industry to another, but a simple example will show how powerful this new tax approach will be on the new prices we will be asked to pay. A current retail price of $10.00 plus sales tax of 7 percent actually comes to $10.70. With their lower government cost overheads and reduced inventory expenses, many businesses will now be able to price the same item at $6.00. *This means that with a new sales tax rate as high as 75 percent, the new real price of $10.50 will actually be smaller.*

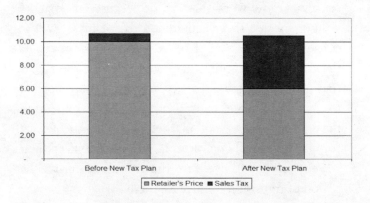

The prices of businesses that sell us products will be more affected like this example than will those of firms that provide us services. The latter will not experience lower inventory costs from their suppliers to the same extent as the former, plus services are generally not subject to sales taxes at this time. However, services often involve relatively more labor which will further reduce their tax overheads, and many governments are quickly moving to add sales taxes to them.

From the standpoint of maintaining competition within similar types of businesses and industries, these variations will be less important because individual firms tend to be more alike in their cost structures.

The essential idea here is simply that overall price changes seen by us as individual consumers will not be the drastic increase scenario that we might otherwise expect when we first begin to think about much larger sales tax rates.

In fact, many cases will result where the total new price will change very little or even go down as enough time passes for our businesses to project and experience much lower costs in their operations.

Of course, these price decreases will not occur simply because we wish them or because our system's design means they should do so. Unless we as consumers make sure that we buy only from sellers that implement significant price decreases, the fact is that most businesses—particularly those most isolated from the ultimate consumer and those possessing the greatest degrees of market power or the fewest competitors—will do everything they can to keep their current prices and even use the confusion during the period of transition to increase them.

As consumers, we can do a great deal to help these businesses behave by using two key facts to decide from whom we will buy.

First, the costs that are important to the prices of any business are not those they have already spent but those that are coming. Therefore, since they will know that lower government taxes and supplier prices are ahead for them, they should start their own price reductions before the transition begins!

Second, our transition approach that gradually moves everyone—including the buyers for businesses such as wholesalers and retailers as well as the ultimate consumers—from the current system of taxes to our new plan will allow all of us to adjust at a better pace and learn as we do so. Our well-designed system will provide that accurate, detailed, and speedy information on the pace of actual price changes be made easily available to all of us as we prepare to enter and go through the transition and for a reasonable period of years after it is completed. This information will include not only average prices and price changes for all types of goods and services in the nation and by region, state, and locale; it will also name specific industries, manufacturers, wholesalers, distributors, retailers, and other such sellers with their actual prices[34], price comparisons to averages for like goods and services, and other information such as price changes since the transition began.

34　As used here, the word price must include *all* the elements that affect a buyer's final cost. These elements consist of (but are not limited to) the actual price, any discounts and rebates or otherwise offsetting amounts for other products and services, payment terms, interest charges (or lack thereof) on time payment arrangements, contractual obligations, installation and setup charges, disconnection and buyback charges, and any other related agreements which may be made between the seller and the buyer.

With this type of information, buyers for businesses such as wholesalers and retailers will be able to make better-informed purchases so that their firms can offer reduced prices to their customers. Each of us as the final consumer can be sure to buy whenever possible only from those businesses that are passing along the cost savings they are experiencing as the transition moves along.

It is important to remember that we must, in every way possible, avoid the trap of implementing price controls, and we need to respect as much as possible the right of any business to keep its own internal information confidential, if it feels the need to do so[35].

Nevertheless, for the temporary period of one year prior to and during the transition, this information regarding prices—which is essentially information that is external to any firm—is so vital to the nation that we must implement the necessary legal powers to compel each and every seller to make it routinely available to an *independent* special commission to be established by Congress. This commission's purpose will be to educate consumers about the art of how sellers design their prices and then to provide the data needed for us to make informed purchasing decisions.

---

35 The desire of a business to keep its information confidential should not be a major obstacle even though some firms and their attorneys have been known to get rather extreme. Such was the case in an early-1997 news story of a nationwide electronics retailer who charged a customer with trespassing because that individual actually used a pad and pen to write down the store's various prices for later and more accurate comparison with other competitors' charges.

Finally, the before-sales tax prices of goods and services should not only decrease during the period of our transition but should generally remain at the new, lower levels after that period is completed. To help ensure this actually happens, our special commission must continue its role and retain its temporary powers to compel pricing information for a reasonable time of two additional years.

This should help prevent sudden returns to old pricing habits and levels that can be possible in the case of some very large businesses and powerful industries. Otherwise, they will use their vast financial resources to survive the transition period and then—if buyers and consumers no longer have the benefit of good information about their actions—simply begin to reestablish their previous higher prices.

Social Security and Medicare Under Our New Tax Approach

Far too many of us have trusted our politicians and have no choice but to rely on the Social Security and Medicare plans of today. Whether right or wrong, these programs represent commitments made by our government and on which many people and families, too far along in life to develop new retirement resources, have relied.

Consequently, these important programs simply cannot be swept away.

We owe our fellow citizens now (or soon to begin) receiving these benefits the assurance that this great nation will honor these commitments.

Our new tax system will make no changes for those citizens already receiving benefits. It will also not change the rules for citizens who will become eligible within the next ten years unless they and their spouses voluntarily agree to do so.

Payments to these individuals will come from the existing trust funds for Social Security and for Medicare until the assets in these funds are used up. After that, (and for as long as needed), all payments will come from the Federal Reserve account for economic downturns.

Citizens who choose not to be covered by Social Security or Medicare plus all others of us whose eligibility for these plans' benefits is more than ten years in the future will have amounts equal to 10 percent of their own plus a portion[36] of their employers' actual past investments in these two trust funds transferred on July 1 of each of the ten years following the start of our transition from the current tax systems. This will be accomplished by having each individual select from a menu of retirement-appropriate investment plans

---

36 Considering the employers' contributions as the employee's investment earnings would cause too great a variation between individuals whose matches had been paid long ago compared to others with only recent payments into the trusts. Therefore, each individual's portion from employers' matching payments will be separately calculated as an amount which equals compounded earnings of 6.0 percent per year on their own payments. Finally, this individual's portion plus their own payments will be added together and become the basis for ten equal annuity transfers to them or their estates.

and having the federal government directly transfer each person's amounts to their designated account and investment company. Once this is done, these funds will be held for retirement purposes and governed by the same kinds of regulations now used for Individual Retirement Accounts.

Since the funds being transferred all originated with previous years' income, none of these amounts will be allowed as credits toward any individual's National Dues. However, the part of each year's annuity attributable to the individual's employers' matches will be included in the individual's High Revenue Tax calculation since that part was originally paid by the employer and no income taxes resulted from those earnings at the time.

At first, these transfer amounts will come from two sources: Half of each year's amounts will be paid by the Social Security and the Medicare trust funds, and 50 percent will come from the federal government's reserve account for economic downturns. Once any trust fund is used up, all remaining payments will come from the Federal Reserve account.

Using Independent Panels of Experts

The use of experts who are independent of political party platforms and partisanship has been widely used in various forms for much of our nation's existence.

One of the first was the establishment of our highest court—the Supreme Court of the United States of America. Here, the expertise is in our constitution and code of laws. The independence of these judges was established by appointments to their jobs that were limited only by good behavior.

Other forms of such panels also exist in bodies like the Federal Reserve Board of Governors, whose expert skills are in the fields of finance and economics. While these governors are certainly subject to pressures that our politicians often direct at them, they are at least technically independent since they cannot be removed during their terms for anything less than the most extreme conditions.

Another way we have used this idea can be seen by how states select and appoint persons to various commissions, such as those who oversee public utilities. In many instances, these states have taken steps to ensure that their commissioners have the needed expertise to deal with the highly technical matters that must be considered if both the consumers and the utilities are to be treated fairly. One method often used is to have the state's governor appoint these commissioners rather than force them to campaign for the electorate's popular vote. Sometimes, the governor is required to choose these appointees from lists submitted by others with names of candidates who are qualified by experience and education to be called an expert in the necessary or specified fields of endeavor.

Many outstanding decisions have been made over the years by such independent panels of experts simply because they possessed the requisite knowledge *and* they were also able to remain generally unaffected by political opinions being voiced by others on the matter. *Unfortunately, it is easy to see that our elected officials could never have been able to make many of those more difficult decisions due simply to the subsequent political consequences.*

Recognizing that even these panels of experts will not be perfect, we can nevertheless draw on this tremendous amount of experience, understanding, and wisdom to make our nation even stronger than it is today. We can do this by using these experts' great value in those limited situations where the otherwise marvelous strengths of our political system for governing are not at their best. Coupling this opportunity with today's more advanced academic and technological abilities, it can be done with very little threat to the powers we voters retain and those we grant to our elected representatives.

- Using today's ever-growing and improving academic and technological abilities, we will be able to vastly improve many of the judgments that are no longer handled well under our current state of political representation, with its dependence on the money and other influences from special interest groups and lobbyists. Also, we will be able to enhance the real independence of experts when making these judgments truly non-political—*or at least much more so than today's approaches.*

- At the same time, we will still be giving very important roles to our elected representatives. They will be the ones who set the larger goals and criteria in advance and who determine the type and makeup of the experts to be used. Finally, the officials that we elect will be responsible for those actions required following any judgments made by these panels of experts.

An example of this greater use of independent experts working within our new tax system will be the panel responsible for determining the necessary amount that is required during a certain year in the federal government's reserve fund for economic downturns.

The type of expertise required will be set out by our Congress, together with the nation's financial and economic goals plus other fundamental criteria—similar to the process used today by a mutual fund to inform potential investors of the conditions and risks to be expected if they invest in that fund. This provides the basis for mutual fund managers to be held accountable for their fiduciary responsibilities as they subsequently make the buying and selling decisions necessary in their work.

The financial and economic goals and other fundamental criteria will be established by our elected officials before any panel can do its work. The goals will have to be technical but general in form, and they cannot contain any politically partisan directives. Finally, our federal courts will be required to automatically review them and invalidate any specific line items within these rules that may be politically partisan[37] or that do not meet appropriate fiduciary standards.

In this example we should expect that the necessary fields of expertise, for any panelist would be financial planning and economics. To find the potential panelists for this job, the nation will look to those professional

---

37   Any provision that may be construed to benefit a particular company or industry *and* not required for national security would be an example of a politically partisan item.

associations who have established standards (such as that for being recognized as a Certified Public Accountant) designed to promote professionalism in a large number of individuals in the fields of either financial planning or economics.

From the membership of these associations, those individuals who have passed their standards examinations will be identified. Then on a regular basis they will be provided with data issued by appropriate government *and* private organizations so they can judge whether or not they believe the financial and economic goals and other criteria established for the Federal Reserve account are being met. With this data and on a regularly scheduled date or when an emergency need is identified, they will all vote electronically *and privately* to determine this account's required level.

Each electronic vote will be received in a computer system with safeguards to prevent tampering by others. The computer programs will then randomly select a statistically necessary number from all the experts casting a vote for that particular event, and it will tally the secret votes of the selected ones into a final result.

Neither any government official nor even the potential panelists themselves will be allowed to find out which individual experts' votes actually went into the final result. When the next occasion for a new vote comes about, the same process will be used, but it will be extremely unlikely that the same individuals' votes will once again be selected by the computer system.

This process will go far not only to protect the privacy and professional integrity of the individual panelists but to greatly dilute the very dangerous and undue power of special interest politicians[38] and lobbyists. *There should be no way they will know which individual voters the computer will select and no reasonable way for these politicians and lobbyists to wield their "charms" on all the many potential panelists located throughout the nation.*

Different panels will have completely different types and mixes of experts and will be determined by the fields of expertise established ahead of time by our elected officials. For example, a local panel in the area of education might be specified to include experts from among experienced educators plus a group of parents of schoolchildren. Finally, for balance, another group of general citizens with business experience might be included.

When votes are actually taken, the computer will be programmed to follow the criteria previously set by that locale's school board. For example, it will accept and record all of the votes cast and then randomly and statistically select the votes of only eight of the educators,

---

38   The term *special interest politician* is simply this writer's way of describing elected officials who cater to a special interest group (such as a certain industry, a particular union or even the political party who helped them get elected) more than the voters that put them in office. In this writer's opinion, the recent case of a United States Senator who promised during his campaign to support a balanced budget amendment appeared to be a special interest politician when he voted against that amendment and gave every appearance that he did so simply because of his party leadership's pressure on him to insure that bill's failure by the margin of his single vote.

eight of the parents, and twelve of the general citizens. Finally, the computer will tally the twenty-eight votes selected and provide the necessary *composite* result only. To further preserve the independence of this panel, no identification of how either the individuals whose votes were randomly selected or the results within the three groups will be made public.

Minimizing Gamesmanship By Government Officials

As used here, the term *gamesmanship* refers to any officials' action taken or practice followed routinely that has an underlying motive, whether overt or covert, to set a budget too low (or too high) and thereby misstate the portion of National Dues that should come from the residents of their jurisdiction[39]. Unfortunately, it seems that virtually all of us believe this kind of thing, whether done deliberately or because of innocent but less-than-professional abilities, occurs far too often today.

---

39   Deliberately or innocently setting budgets too high is also a type of gamesmanship that needs to be eliminated, and the comparisons of similar state and local averages will show us when and where it occurs. This evidence for local voters, plus the author's belief that our new tax approach adequately handles the most serious negative effects on those of us who reside elsewhere, means that automatic reductions in sales taxes otherwise due are not needed.

It is easy enough to understand why an elected or appointed official will be tempted to underestimate a budget. Not wanting to hassle with constituents who expect lower taxes is one very powerful political reason to take such an approach. However, if this was allowed to become too prevalent under our new tax approach it could create significant problems for those of us who live elsewhere by creating inappropriately large refunds for the original jurisdiction's residents and smaller-than-needed National Sales Tax percentages for everyone.

Our new tax system will reduce the revenues due to any government body *whenever the results of their actions show that this type of gamesmanship appears to be present*. Such an adjustment will *not* be affected by any question of why the government officials for that body allowed this condition to exist, since the results of either deliberate *or* innocent gamesmanship—if left unchecked—will be damaging to the rest of us in other states and locales whose officials did their work properly.

While other groups may be interested in the more partisan attempts to determine whether any apparent gamesmanship was taken for good or bad motives, whether or not it was done in the public eye or if it simply happened because of unforeseeable circumstances versus a lack of professionalism on the part of the official's staff, our tax plan must and will be concerned only with correcting the results in ways that will provide powerful incentives for this to be done more professionally in future years.

The means for these corrections to occur will be very simple and *automatic*. National Dues refunds and payments for each state and local government jurisdiction will be compared annually with average refund and payment amounts owed in all states and in all localities. From this comparison, the amount of statistical deviation from these averages for other jurisdictions of comparable population will be determined for each local and state government body.

Then each state and locale with refunds exceeding these averages by more than 3 percent will automatically receive a reduced amount of National Sales Tax distributions than they would be due if their budget estimates had shown fewer indications of apparent gamesmanship.

For example, if a large state's average refund exceeded the average of all other similarly large states by 3.2 percent, this state's sales tax distributions will be reduced by 1.0 percent. If a second large state's above-average refund varied by an even greater 5.1 percent, its sales tax distributions will be reduced by 4.0 percent.

Like corrections will apply for state and local government bodies with lower-than-average National Dues payments displaying similar excessive deviations.

Both corrections will apply using an increasing scale that equates the percentages after 6.0 percent in refund deviations.

All amounts withheld from any state or local government will become part of the federal reserve accounts for economic downturns and wartime.

These types of corrections will not apply to the federal budget because of:

1. The extreme importance of its primary budget objectives of national defense (so each of us

will remain free and more secure) and promoting commerce (so all of us will have more job opportunities)

2. Our national need to eliminate (or at least minimize) public debt at so high a level of government

3. The negative effects of any gamesmanship at the federal level will be shared equally by each of us—its citizens—wherever we may reside

This is not to say that local and state budgets are unimportant. They are very important! However, items in a local or state budget will not have the dire consequences for *all* of us that a major breakdown in our national defense would produce. The same is true to only a slightly lesser extent of the effects on *all* of us if a failure occurs in our systems designed to promote better commerce throughout our nation. Further, our new tax plan provides another means to local and state governments for handling their short-term budget difficulties. The optional local sales tax for limited periods of time gives them such an opportunity, while at the same time alerting the local or state electorate that they need to undertake their own corrections.

Implementing Our New Tax Approach through a Transition Plan

So many changes must occur under our new tax plan that it is not realistic or desirable for the nation to try to move through them in a single event or date. Instead, it will be far better for us to step through them over a reasonable period of several years. During that time, these changes will happen in a more gradual fashion giving us and our organizations needed time to adjust as we each learn how to live and work within the new system.

A good example of this can be seen by considering the changes that our businesses will have to understand and accomplish to revise and reduce the prices of their goods and services to their customers. So much will depend on the actions and reactions of everyone— starting with each being able to plan with confidence on all government taxes and fees being reduced on a known schedule.

Knowing this schedule will allow all businesses to begin the first price reductions shortly before the actual transition period begins. Basic businesses (such as manufacturers and shopping center landlords) and service firms (such as stockbrokers or advertising companies and medical practices) will be able to act more quickly. Companies such as wholesalers and retailers that buy inventory goods from them will also be able to reduce prices before the transition starts but will have to be slightly more tentative. These latter businesses' initial price reductions can come about based on the known government plans plus estimates of their suppliers' price reductions. However, further decreases will be easier only after they actually see the level of change from their inventory suppliers and services they use— such as advertising, rents, utilities, and cleaning.

Both as individual taxpayers and as owners and employees, we will want this to happen in a reasonably ordered fashion. This way our jobs will remain intact, and the regular increases in sales tax rates will be steadily offset by simultaneous decreases in these businesses' portions of their prices.

An effective transition plan will work as follows:

(a) National per capita dues and credits, National Sales Tax rates, and High Revenue Taxes will be established for the first year of transition in exactly the same way they will be done in the fifth and subsequent years when the change is complete. At the same time, all current tax plans will also remain in effect. Then, during that first year, both types of taxes and tax returns will be used, except that each individual, family, and organization will pay only 80 percent of any taxes (including any existing state and local sales taxes) owed under the current system, plus 20 percent due under the new approach.

- Tax revenues generated under the new approach will start being distributed immediately to the federal, state, and local governments in amounts equal to 20 percent of those calculated as due if the transition were complete. Also, these government bodies will each be required to begin funding their reserve accounts to reach by the year's end levels of 20 percent of that which would be required if the transition were complete.

- Payroll withholding amounts, estimated tax payments by individuals subject to such procedures, and all other processes for paying our governments as the year proceeds will be calculated under the rules of our current tax system. Only 80 percent of those amounts will be withheld or payable.

(b) This procedure will be repeated in the second year of the transition period, except that each individual and organization will pay only 60 percent of all amounts due under the current tax systems plus 40 percent of any calculated amounts due under the new tax plan.

(c) In the third and fourth years of the transition, each individual and organization will pay 40 percent and 20 percent respectively of all amounts due under the current tax systems. In these same years, amounts calculated under the new tax approach will be due at the levels of 60 percent and 80 percent respectively.

(c) Beginning with the fifth year, the transition period will be complete for all tax items, and individuals, families, and organizations will neither pay nor file any tax returns for that (or future) years under the now old tax systems. Only amendments to previous years' returns, disputes, back taxes owed but not yet settled and any other such unresolved items will still have to be settled under the old systems' laws and rules in effect at the time they arose.

Only two exceptions will exist to this transition plan. The first will apply for those businesses with major portions of their sales from our most basic industries of farming, mining, and manufacturing from raw materials.

Because the prices charged by these firms to their customers play such an important role in the ultimate cost of finished goods and services to the final consumer, it will be better for them to make the transition slightly ahead of all other organizations and individuals. In this way, their new and lower prices will work through the nation's economy faster and *help* speed forward the same desired results for all other types of businesses who are more closely tied to the ultimate consumers.

Under this exception, large farms with annual sales of $10,000,000.00 or more in the last year before the transition begins, plus all businesses engaged in mining or manufacturing from raw materials, will be required to complete the transition one year faster than the majority of us[40]. Their tax payments owed under the current systems will be payable at the rates of 75 percent, 50 percent, 25 percent, and 0 percent in the first, second, third, and fourth years respectively. At the same time, their tax payments calculated under the new tax approach will be due at the rates of 25 percent, 50 percent, 75 percent, and 100 percent in the first, second, third, and fourth years respectively.

The second exception will affect each of us with any of the presently allowed tax deferred savings plans such as Individual Retirement Accounts, Keogh accounts, and 401(k) funds. It will also affect those fewer numbers of us with dollars set aside through various types of deferred income plans to the extent that taxes (that would have otherwise been due at the time this income was set aside) have not already been paid.

All of these accounts will be allowed to continue under the rules and regulations in effect on the day

---

40 This faster transition will *not* apply to their tax and workers compensation obligations paid on behalf of employees. All of these types of payments—such as unemployment, social security and Medicare taxes—and employee withholding amounts will follow the slower transition schedule.

before we begin the transition to our new tax approach. Then, as these funds are withdrawn by their owners, they will be included in the individual's High Revenue Tax calculations since no income taxes were paid on them at the time or on their earnings during the interim years.

ADDENDUM 1

HOW WE CAN GET
THERE FROM HERE!

Political Reality—1776 and Today

The "American Dream" was formally written and codified in 1776 in the Declaration of Independence and slightly more than a decade later in the Constitution of the United States of America with its Bill of Rights. *What marvelous documents these were—then and now—for their wisdom and far-sightedness. They also were—and are— just as marvelous for their very strong dedication to a belief in the "people's" ability to understand issues and to "do the right thing."* Obviously, these documents were produced by people like us who had real human imperfections. It seems equally clear to any of us who look hard at these and their associated writings (like *The Federalist Papers*) that they were produced because these imperfect people thought and acted with a high degree of *statesmanship* (which here is defined as "the art of exercising political leadership wisely and without narrow partisanship"[41]).

---

41 Actually, this definition is slightly paraphrased (or derived) from the 1974 edition of Webster's *New Collegiate Dictionary* definition of Statesman.

However, in the opinion of this author (and apparently many other citizens as well), *a huge change has taken over our nation's political landscape between that time and the present!* Sometime during that interval, we reached a point where the vast majority of our government officials no longer feel the importance of that kind of statesmanship and where doing what the country needs is not why most of these people believe they were elected. *Instead, what seems to be most important today is the accumulation and exercise of power by the individual or political party. Truth—on the part of a politician, a bureaucrat, or a lobbyist—is unnecessary so long as their answers can be given a spin that sounds good to the public.*

Much of the power exercised by today's politicians, bureaucrats, special interest groups, and their lobbyists originate in the vast amounts of information that our governments now hold on each of us. *The greatest source of this power is probably the vast and complicated web of laws, rules, regulations, and requirements—often conflicting with one another—that our governments have laid on each of us, our enterprises, and our personal wealth.* Anyone or any family who dares to work hard and rise even a little above a condition of just getting by or living from payday to payday quickly finds that it will require an army of lawyers, accountants, and other professionals to keep their legal, tax, financial, and business affairs from running afoul of the system.

And as soon as one (with or without lawyers, account- ants, and other professionals) gets everything in order, the politicians, bureaucrats, and special interest groups add new laws, rules, and regulations that change things so that the game starts all over.

Even if those who dare to rise manage to follow all these laws, rules, and regulations with honest intent, a simple mistake on a tax form or a payment mailed on time (but lost by the government's mailroom) is quickly followed by form letters demanding late payment plus penalties and interest charges that can ruin a good reputation or a well-founded business just getting started.

In today's government, few old laws or systems that were good in the past—or were just not good from their inception—are repealed. Instead, new modifications or amendments are added to fix the fresh problems they have created or exposed. Old government agencies that may have been needed during or after a major event such as World War II simply continue to function or are continually altered just to keep them long past their need[42]. Then, on top of these old laws and agencies that are no longer applicable to the times, our government officials simply pile on us new laws, rules, and regulations.

This works very well for these officials because the added complications and resulting confusion by the nation's citizens creates real power for those elected, appointed, or otherwise employed by our governments. Not coincidentally, it also works very well for special interest groups and large organizations with their high-paid lobbyists. The

---

42   Most of us will also realize that too many politicians and government operations really believe that their main purpose is to create governmental jobs—and thereby (in their mind) make at least some voters more indebted to them or reduce unemployment. When this is the case, their efforts become directed not at serving their customers and citizens, but at maintaining the maximum number of government employees no matter what the cost and how poor the service provided.

complications and confusion generated allows them to use their influence and money (such as political action contributions) to get our elected officials and their appointees to bury within the complex wording of so many laws, rules, and regulations vast numbers of special provisions that give those companies, causes, and industries unwarranted favors and advantages.

Considering this, there should be no surprise when our officials continually fail to pass such things as real campaign reform or that they feel the way to repair a problem in our tax codes is to add some new provision rather than eliminate old ones. *Job security for a politician or a lobbyist actually increases by continually adding complexity to a government's laws, rules, and regulations. Reducing this complexity lessens their power and the advantages gained by their clients. In particular, letting citizens remain free to operate with personal solutions and resources reduces the politician's power over us and our lives. For many politicians—this may be their worst nightmare!*

Political Power and Our New Tax Approach

Politicians and bureaucrats will interpret our new tax plan as one that drastically reduces their personal power, even though what it actually does is move their roles back and up toward that of statesmen and stateswomen, which is a very vital (and thus powerful) position for this nation. They will also proclaim loudly that it will greatly dilute their political party's power.

Large organizations (such as a major manufacturing company or a national charity) and special interest groups (such as an industry association, large trade union, or environmental coalition) with their highly-paid lobbyists will find our new tax plan extremely undesirable. They will see it as one that significantly limits their market powers against smaller competitors. They will also see that it will reduce their ability to use influence and money to gain special concessions and favors hidden in the fine print of many laws, rules, and regulations that often deal with totally different subjects.

Some non-profit and tax-exempt organizations will even find our new tax plan objectionable because it means competitors will gain many of the same financial advantages they now have to themselves.

Federal, state, and local public employees will oppose it after being told over and over how it will cause their jobs to disappear. *They will mistakenly believe this, despite the fact that the vast majority of their jobs actually depend not on how we pay but primarily on how much is asked of our government and how well they do those things.* A relatively small percentage of present government workers such as tax appraisers and much of the present Internal Revenue Service, with its state and local counterparts, will no longer be necessary. The far greater numbers of productive workers, such as law enforcement officers, park rangers, military, highway engineers, social caseworkers, secretaries, computer programmers, and office staffs will continue just as they do now.

When today's massive, complex, and often conflicting sets of tax laws, rules, and regulations are eliminated in favor of a far simpler code with fewer loopholes or judgment calls (such as property appraisals of our homes for tax purposes), *and* when huge files of extremely personal information on the vast majority of us can no longer be justified, the present power of our politicians and bureaucrats will have been altered more than too many of them will willingly accept. Of even more importance, today's large organizations, foreign countries, and special interest groups who now are able to so easily use their money to "work the system" and gain favorable treatment for their industry, firm, nation, or cause will have actually lost huge amounts of power.

For all these reasons, our current and aspiring politicians, bureaucrats, large organizations, and special interest groups will create unbelievable numbers of objections, practice foot-dragging and gridlock, and even sabotage on our new tax plan. Still more sinister reasons—such as our new tax approach's huge reduction in any real need to keep personal files on individual citizens—will cause far too many of our officials to literally fight this change if not overtly, then covertly.

Making Our New Tax Approach Happen

Our politicians, bureaucrats, large organizations, special interest groups and their lobbyists have clearly accumulated unbelievable amounts of power since the beginning of the American Dream—especially since the middle of the last century.

Further, these groups are both organized and have learned far better than we want to admit how to use this power to their advantage. How often have we experienced new laws that were advertised as one thing but in reality were later found to have been written (or amended at the last minute) to do the opposite? Have we not elected our officials with sufficient unity and numbers to do a specific task only to have virtually all of them come back telling us how they "voted for that thing but it failed anyway"[43]?

We need to just accept that this power can (and apparently much more often than not) overcome even the most honest and well meaning of us after being elected to it.

---

43   As an example, the majority party in Congress in 1995 and 1996 virtually all claimed to have voted for term limits (as promised in their Contract With America) when they came home to talk to their constituents. But no such legislation was passed despite their voting majority in that session. Most of us probably believe the reason was that no agreement could be reached on whether the actual limits of a Congressional seat's term should be six, eight or twelve years. We can all understand, however, that no sitting Congress member would really want to pass this legislation - unless that member was more of a Statesman than most current-day politicians. Thus, is it possible that someone or their party really worked the system by arranging for enough of those in favor of the "idea" to simply divide their votes between the various numbers of years - whether six, eight or twelve - so that no single plan could get the needed number of votes to pass? If that or something similar did happen, it would then mean that *each Congress member could truthfully report to their voters that they personally supported term limits.*

In another example, the minority party in Congress in 1997 defeated by one vote a constitutional amendment for a balanced budget by using a new Senator who was somehow persuaded to not support it *even though he was elected less than six months earlier apparently in major part because of his promise to do just the opposite*! Had the bill been passed, the amendment would have still required ratification by a large number of states. Were he and his party's leaders not even willing to let the people have the chance to consider something these politicians did not want because it might curtail some of their powers? And did he really represent the voters of his state or was he more in the debt of his party?

Thus, we must not accept any promises or acts in this matter from members of Congress or state governments! It is simply no longer reasonable to expect the necessary numbers of them to willingly give up any of their powers just because it might be the will of the people[44]!

Considering these factors, the needed constitutional amendment cannot be left in the care of our Congress (or career politicians), except where the exact wording of Addendum 2 is used *and* the details in this book are followed *without exception*. With our politicians' vested interests against such a change, *any variation must be considered by the citizens of this nation as unacceptable and potentially designed to subvert the effort.*

This writer prefers that this constitutional amendment be initiated by citizens organizing their efforts in ways similar to California's state tax reduction movement several decades ago and using the exact wording of Addendum 2. This will accomplish the first step, which is to get the necessary two-thirds of our state legislatures to present *precisely the same wording* in applications to the Congress. As spelled out in Article Five of our nation's constitution, that will *require* our federal legislature to "call a convention for

---

44 In the mind of this writer, a legislature consisting of Statesmen and Stateswomen would have acted differently once they saw that they could not agree on the details of the examples in Footnote 43. They would have passed a term limits law which submitted the selection of the number of years to a national referendum by the voters; including (if needed) a runoff ballot between the two plans receiving the most votes in the first round. And they would have passed a balanced budget amendment plan that the citizens could then have debated and voted for or against. Real Statesmen and Stateswomen would have entrusted this much of their power to the people.

proposing amendments." Further, each state's citizen movement should be certain that their legislature specify in every such application to the Congress that the desire of the citizens is for the mode of ratification to be by state conventions rather than state legislatures. *Then—so long as control of this convention is not allowed by professionals frequently or currently in office or involved with national, state or local politics—variations from Addendum 2 should be debated and included in the final version to be submitted for ratification by the subsequent state conventions[45].*

---

45 Several reasons exist in the mind of this writer for being so specific about the process. First, as noted earlier, allowing this to be done by existing or future politicians in Washington simply dictates that we not give them any freedom whatsoever to change anything in the wording of Addendum 2. They are too far removed from those who elected them, too subject to the agenda of their party's leaders (see again Footnote 43 and especially its second example), and they are too much an easy target for so many powerful special interests with high-paid lobbyists. In short, the more this action can be accomplished by ordinary citizens and away from The Congress (and the state legislatures who also often have an overabundance of lobbyist input), the better will be our chances true debate can occur since the convention delegates will be too numerous, not nearly so well-known, and thus more difficult for partisan party leaders plus the special interest groups and lobbyists to work their magic!

Second, being specific provides a common plan for something that will have to occur in at least 34 different states at about the same time. Finally, having every state effort follow the exact wording in Addendum 2 should make it less difficult to keep all these separate efforts synchronized *until* The Congress is forced to call a convention. However, *once that critical step is done and cannot be reversed, variations which improve the wording of Addendum 2 should be considered in direct proportion to the degree that "ordinary" citizens who are not professional politicians manage and direct this national convention.*

ADDENDUM 2

ARTICLE (NUMBER)
CONSTITUTION OF THE UNITED STATES OF AMERICA
(PROPOSED)[46]

Section 1. The Sixteenth Article of Amendment to the Constitution of the United States of America is hereby repealed.

Section 2. The Congress shall have the duty and power without fail to establish and fully fund from its appropriate revenue sources in Sections 4, 5, 6, 7, and 8

---

46 *This proposed amendment cannot belong solely to any partisan party—Democratic, Libertarian, Reform, Republican, or other. In fact, it is and must remain in every way strictly nonpartisan. Because Addendum 2 is part of a volume which is fully copyrighted (with all rights reserved), permission is hereby granted for anyone to copy or use this proposed Constitutional amendment addendum only so long as no partisan claims are attached to its use.*

of this article a reserve revenue account for use during periods of general economic stress as determined by independent panels of economics and financial experts' judgments relating to sound financial practices. Elected officials shall be able to access this reserve account only during such specific periods and only in amounts determined by each such panel. The Congress shall have the additional duty and power without fail to establish and fully fund from their appropriate revenue sources in Sections 4, 5, 6, 7, and 8 of this article a reserve revenue account for use only during periods of war when requested by The President and declared by the Congress. These duties shall constitute a specific fiduciary responsibility on each elected individual in the Congress for which failure shall require automatic lifetime removal from Congress.

Section 3. The Congress shall have the duty and power to establish annually the complete operating budget for use by the nation and funded only from their appropriate sources. It shall be a primary duty without fail of Congress to publish and make widely available in detailed, but easily understandable form to its electorate by August 1 of the preceding year its complete and total operations and capital accounts budget proposed for the coming year in very straightforward summary and line item formats specifically set up to facilitate its electorate's knowledge and understanding of their planned budget. Each such proposed budget shall be finalized and approved by the following August 31 or required to be established at a level equal to 95 percent of the current year's budget, and published by the following October 1 in both total and per capita amounts in national tables by the federal operation established in accordance with Section 10 of this article.

Section 4. The Congress shall have the duty and power to establish annual dues for each citizen plus other individuals living in the United States of America, but excluding each citizen on active duty in the nation's military forces or designated national volunteer organizations. Such dues shall be the daily prorated portion of the coming year's annual budget per capita amount for each individual except that children under two years of age shall not be included and children between two and eighteen years of age shall be counted at the rate of 50 percent. The Congress shall also have the duty and power to establish a two-part system of credits for personal expenditures by individual citizens which will allow each to reduce their dues amount otherwise payable and earn a payment. The first of these credit parts shall be established as percentages of each individual's or immediate family's particular National Dues amount, shall apply only to basic living needs and shall enable such individuals or immediate family to reduce their National Dues by up to 90 percent. This credit part shall further include credits for adult's volunteer work performed and children's school achievement under standards established by the Congress which when combined with their Basic Living Credits shall enable individuals or families to reduce their annual National Dues up to 100 percent and thereafter provide citizens or citizen families to earn a payment of up to 15 percent of their National Dues. The second of these credit parts shall be established as specific amounts, shall apply only to investments that create jobs, encourage education and charity, protect and build long-term individual health and financial security, and shall enable individuals to reduce their annual National Dues by up to 100 percent when combined with credits for basic living needs.

Section 5. The Congress shall have the duty and power to establish a single National Sales Tax on all commercial, government, and other transactions involving goods and services sold, rented, or otherwise conveyed to final consumers; excepting only certain essential goods and services determined by the Congress to be necessary food staples, housing and utilities, essential insurance, education, savings and investments, essential healthcare and dependent care; and excepting certain goods and services which it designates as potentially highly costly or otherwise detrimental to the nation's health or children and on which it establishes individually appropriate multiples of this otherwise single National Sales Tax to be collected. This duty and power shall create for each member of the Congress a fiduciary responsibility to establish the actual level of each year's National Sales Tax estimated as adequate for but sufficient only to meet the total of the federal operating budget, including specific 2 percent funds each for special needs of urban-poor and of rural situations, for the coming year set in accordance with Section 3 of this article, and after appropriate consideration of all other revenue sources, reserve requirements and federal debt in accordance with Sections 2, 4, 6, 7, and 8 of this article.

Section 6. The Congress shall have the duty and power to establish an additional High Revenue Tax on individual and organization revenues which, after deducting any cost of domestic materials or inventory expenses, any contributions to bona-fide churches and charities, and limited costs of wages plus training of any individual citizen, are in excess of levels determined every third year or during wartime by an independent panel of economics experts as most appropriate for the nation to equalize market power and economic opportunities between all individuals and between large and small organizations while preserving national security. These High Revenue Taxes shall be levied without variations between like parties on their consolidated revenues considering any and all related income, significant ties with other individuals, organizations and wealth producing activities with which each party may have interests.

Section 7. The Congress shall have the duty and power to establish means for the government to assess additional charges strictly limited to optional services provided directly to final consumers, to levy fines for civil and criminal actions, and to seize property and other assets as allowed by duly enacted criminal laws, and the Congress shall have the power to levy tariffs on non-domestic goods and services upon entry or delivery to points within the United States of America. Such additional taxes, charges, fines, seized property and assets, and tariffs together with any other forms of miscellaneous revenues shall belong exclusively to the economic stress reserve fund of the United States of America.

Section 8. Except during periods of war when requested by the President and declared by the Congress, the Congress shall have no power to establish or collect any other forms of revenue generation schedules on individuals or organizations except as set forth in Sections 4, 5, 6, and 7 of this article.

Section 9. Each state and officially constituted local government with elected officials shall be able to participate with the federal system established by this article provided they enact and follow within their individual jurisdiction the exact and total requirements of this article. In such cases they shall promptly receive their proportionate shares of the National Sales Tax, the High Revenue Tax, and they shall have the additional power to establish an optional local sales tax within their jurisdiction only. Any such optional sales tax amounts shall be applicable only to those transactions established by the Congress in accordance with Section 5 of this article and which occur wholly within that jurisdiction. They shall also promptly receive any funds resulting from goods and services provided by any state or local government or semi-government body specifically constituted for the provision of such goods and services exclusively for the reserve fund of the state or local government that established that body. Any such optional sales tax amounts may be established for no more or less than an additional 10 percent for periods of no more or less than two calendar years, and may not be extended except by local electorate approval for each such two years extension. This prompt receipt of the above proportionate shares shall be done as provided in Section 10 of this article. No non-participating state or its local governments or its citizens shall receive any disbursements from the National Dues, the National Sales Tax, or the High Revenue Tax.

Section 10. The Congress shall have the duty of establishing economically sound criteria for the prompt collection and distribution of appropriate portions of all tax and other revenues collected in accordance with Sections 4, 5, 6, 7, 8, and 9 of this article including to each of the participating several States and each officially constituted participating local government with elected officials using an approach that recognizes the priority claim of the federal budget, the special needs of urban-poor and rural areas within the nation and a requirement for overall balance between population and location of economic activity. The Congress shall have the additional duty and power of funding the single government operation responsible for the collection of all taxes and other forms of assets and revenues as set forth in Sections 4, 5, 6, 7, 8, and 9 of this article, and their timely and prompt distribution of appropriate collected portions of these revenues which belong to each of the participating States and to each participating officially constituted local government with elected officials except that no State or local government shall be entitled to any distribution which exceeds that jurisdiction's final budget amount for the year as approved in accordance with Section 3 of this article and may be limited to reduced levels in the subsequent year if evidence shows any such jurisdiction's average dues payments or refunds vary from the overall average of like jurisdictions beyond limits established by the Congress with the purpose of providing strong incentives for accurate budgeting processes by all jurisdictions. This government operation shall function under the direction of the Executive Branch of the United States of America as the single point of contact for all individuals and organizations in all tax matters including collection, refunds and disputes, as well as publication and making easily available throughout the nation all finalized budget and per capita amounts tables as set forth in Section 3 of this article.

Section 11. This article shall become effective on January 1 following its ratification as an amendment to the Constitution of the United States of America, and shall be instituted during a transition period not to exceed four years from that date. During this transition period, the Congress and each of the several States, each officially constituted local government with elected officials and each officially empowered governmental and semi-governmental body within a state electing to participate as outlined in Section 9 above shall retain their previous powers to implement any programs existing at least two years prior to this article's ratification date except that any basic alteration to such programs' structure, size or revenue needs is prohibited unless approved by a two-thirds majority of the appropriate electorate. Further, during this transition period the actual revenue generation resulting from the individual previous powers retained shall be reduced annually by the transition period's percentages of 20 percent, or 25 percent when applied to individuals and organizations engaged in large farms or basic mining and manufacturing. Also during this transition period, the actual revenue generation from each individual and organization subject to Sections 2,

3, 4, 5, 6, 7, 8, and 9 of this article shall be increased each year by a level of 20 percent when applied to individuals and organizations not engaged in large farms or basic mining and manufacturing, or 25 percent when applied to individuals and organizations engaged in large farms or basic mining and manufacturing.

Section 12. During the period of transition in accordance with Section 11 of this article plus the up to one year immediately preceding and the two years immediately following, the Congress shall have the duty and power to establish and adequately fund a fully independent and sufficient special commission of economic advisors to educate consumers and report weekly to the citizens and consumers of the United States of America on the status of and changes in the individual and industry-wide prices, terms and other such relevant data and actions of any and all sellers and suppliers of goods and services before, during and after the transition period. Such sellers and suppliers shall be required to cooperate fully and promptly with all requests from this special commission who shall use prices and pricing information so furnished and who shall have sufficient investigative powers and immunity from damages to carry out its role in a timely manner. This special commission and its duty and powers may be extended by Congress for an additional period of up to two years should Congress decide conditions at the time warrant such a limited extension.

About the Author

After four years in the United States Navy assigned to the nuclear submarine program in Washington, DC, Robert Savage spent almost thirty years with Southern Bell in Florida as a marketing manager and as an account manager to NASA during the Apollo/Saturn Moon program; for AT&T in New York and New Jersey as a nationwide pricing manager; and for BellSouth as a pricing director and rate case witness for Florida, Georgia, North Carolina, and South Carolina.

Since 1989 he and his wife Annette have co-owned The Toy School®, which was established in Atlanta. This small retail store operated successfully for eleven years, winning three major awards (Playthings Magazine's international merchandising achievement recognition in 1991 and 1992, as well as Atlanta Magazine's "Best Toy Store" in 1994). It continues now as The Toy School Corner in Georgia and South Carolina.

Bob is currently the executive director of a startup 501(c)(3)—the American Foundation for Furthering Ideas that Rekindle the Miracle of 1776 (AFFIRM1776). This small nonprofit is envisioned to promote dialogue and critical studies of ideas from ordinary citizens that can help our nation build on and/or return to principles used by our founders in 1776.

Annette and Bob have one son, Robert Keith, and four grandchildren. Both are active members of the First Baptist Church in Hartwell, and he is the treasurer for the local American Legion Post and Rotary Club.